Praise for Eight Questions

"God's ways do not always make sense to us. Sometimes He gives answers, and sometimes He wants us to trust Him with the mystery. *Eight Questions* provides a unique perspective on how to walk with God during those crucial times. The insights shared by Paul will provide encouragement, direction, and perspective. Even more importantly, this book will lead you back to pursuing an intimate relationship with Jesus Christ."

— Dr. Johnny Hunt, Former SBC President
and Senior Pastor of First Baptist Church Woodstock, GA

"I am so thankful for the friendship and partnership in the Gospel with Paul Gotthardt. His understanding of the life of Christ in and through us as believers absolutely hits the target! I strongly recommend this book to anyone desiring to deepen their relationship with Jesus and experience the victory of living life out of the overflow of intimacy with Him."

— Vance Pitman, Senior Pastor of Hope Church in Las Vegas

"While most books go straight to giving us answers, Paul Gotthardt gives us questions. But not just any questions. These are questions that will help you wrestle with God in very personal and practical way. If you are feeling stuck in your faith, *Eight Questions* will guide you into a life changing conversation with God."

— Mac Lake, Chief Launch Officer of The Launch Network

"As a Church Planter and Pastor, Paul Gotthardt has experienced the highs and lows of ministry. This book is a great real life depiction of situations all of us in ministry can relate to as well as the questions we've asked when we're searching for God's answer or plan. Read this book and not only discover *what* Jesus taught, but *how* He taught it!"

—Shane Critser, Team Leader for Church Mobilization
at the North American Mission Board (SBC)

"As I have watched Paul's church over the past 8 years there has been an incredible, and commendable focus on discipleship. The people of Life Baptist Church are taught the Word of God every Sunday and are genuinely maturing into full-fledged disciples of Jesus Christ. This book gives insight to how that has been accomplished in the lives of so many."

— Josh Teis, Lead Pastor of Southern Hills Baptist Church in Las Vegas

"Paul Gotthardt is a great friend and mentor. His passion for helping others experience a life-changing relationship with Jesus is evident from the first time you meet him. I am certain that *Eight Questions* will challenge you in your walk with Jesus and help you discover how He teaches you throughout life's everyday moments."

— Travis Fox, Lead Pastor of Grace City Church in Salt Lake City

"Paul Gotthardt is an incredible communicator, mentor, and friend with a true heart for God and His Kingdom. I recommend this book to anyone that desires a deeper understanding of Jesus' teaching and how His style of teaching is essential to our growth as disciples' of Christ. Paul's book has insightful and practical wisdom for a messy and misguided world."

— Gary Gann, Lead Pastor of Central Southwest in Las Vegas

"I have been following Paul Gotthardt's ministry for the past year, and after looking at *Eight Questions*, my suspicions are confirmed. This man has wrestled with God, and he has gotten some things settled (things that give him insight, passion, and a humble love for his God). If you are yearning for an intimate loving relationship with our purposeful God, take a look at these questions. Go as many rounds with God as it takes to work out the answers for yourself."

— Cheryl Burford, Director of Children's Ministry at Green Valley Baptist in Henderson

"The key to knowing God is to know Jesus Christ. In this book Pastor Paul takes us by the hand and leads us into a greater understanding of our amazing Lord. He shares how Jesus taught His earthly disciples and how He is still teaching us today. Understanding Christ's teaching style helps us overcome much of the mystery, confusion or angst we feel as we follow our Lord. Just know that this author is your friend, and this book can provide insight into this challenging but exciting journey. Enjoy!"

— Bret Holman, Lead Pastor of All People Christian Church in Las Vegas

EIGHT
QUESTIONS
...and the God who's asking.

A guide to living confidently in Christ
when life doesn't make sense.

Paul Gotthardt

WestBow
PRESS
A DIVISION OF THOMAS NELSON

ISBN: 978-1-4497-6811-9 (sc)
ISBN: 978-1-4497-6813-3 (hc)
ISBN: 978-1-4497-6812-6 (e)

Library of Congress Control Number: 2012918113

WestBow Press books may be ordered through booksellers or by contacting:

WestBow Press
A Division of Thomas Nelson
1663 Liberty Drive
Bloomington, IN 47403
www.westbowpress.com
1-(866) 928-1240

Edited by Nicole Lauffer

Book Design by Matt Phillips

Printed in the United States of America

WestBow Press rev. date: 10/24/2012

To Brea,

Your joy is contagious,

Your love for God inspires me,

Your partnership in life
enables me to reach for more.

Table of Contents

Acknowledgements

Eight Questions has one author but many contributors. It is the culmination of God's people investing insights, encouragement, and support into my life at crucial points in the journey. Apart from God's grace, and the encouragement of others, this book would not be possible.

I want to thank my parents, Fred and Gladys Gotthardt, for teaching and modeling a consistent Christian life. You provided a stable, Christ-centered home for your kids, and we are still reaping the benefits of it.

I'm grateful for the support and encouragement of my siblings (Michelle, Alan, and Melissa). Thank you for the prayers, conversations, support, and encouragement over the years.

I am grateful to my mentor, Dr. Johnny Hunt. Among other things, you taught me that ministry runs on the rails of relationships, and you opened my mind to the vastness of God's Kingdom. I will always be grateful for the investment you and FBCW have made in me.

I want to thank Vance Pitman for believing in me as a church planter and entrusting the truths of the Christ-life to me. Were it not for your encouragement and guidance, *8 Questions* would have been *The Memoirs of a Former Church Planter*. Thank you for your friendship and for everything Hope Church has done to make our journey exciting.

I am so thankful for the leadership team at Life. You all make the journey exciting. Philipp Meinecke, you are my "partner in crime" for ministry. You have been with Brea and me since the beginning. This book is a reflection of our journey together. Thank you, Matt Phillips, for being a graphic-design, creative-arts ninja. Everything looks better after you've touched it (including this book). Also, thank you to Jason Battjes and Beth Glassford. I am so grateful for the way you invest in the children, teens, and families at Life. Our church is stronger because of you.

A special thanks goes to Nicole Lauffer for her tireless efforts and amazing editing skills. You have taken my ramblings, en-dashes, and ellipses, and made them readable. Thank you for all you've done.

Thank you to Life Baptist Church. This is our story. You have lived it with me, and I am grateful for the privilege of serving as your pastor.

Finally, I am grateful to God. He has taken difficulty and turned it to an opportunity for growth in Christ. Apart from Him, we exist with moments of happiness. With Him, we live and move and have our being. I am stunned by the wonders of grace.

Introduction

Today, if your life seems like an endless cat and mouse game with God, I understand. If your day is filled with mystical searches for divine clues, I get it. If you find yourself frustrated because you know God is trying to teach you something, but you have no idea what it is, I want to encourage you. You are not alone.

This book will help you develop a listening ear for God's voice, discover areas where God is at work in your life, and deepen your relationship with Christ. You will grow in each of these areas as you explore the teaching styles that Christ used with his disciples. The combination of these discoveries will add incredible value and fulfillment to your relationship with God. Instead of confusion, you can have confidence as you navigate life's challenges. But let's start at the beginning.

While writing this book, I'm thirty-seven years old, and I've spent twenty-six of those years in formal education. Sometimes it seems as though I've spent my entire life in school. I've had my fair share of teachers, professors, instructors, teaching assistants, substitutes, and whomever else they decided to put in a classroom. While I've learned a lot in specific classes, there are at least two concepts that I've learned about education in general.

First, every teacher is different. I'm not talking about being different as a person; I'm talking about being different as a teacher. They emphasize different things. They have different expectations. They have different styles, strengths, and weaknesses. Some are animated and entertaining; others are lifeless and boring. Some stress the lectures; others stress the book. Some are organized; others live in a state of intelligent chaos. They're all different!

Second, you must adjust to their styles of teaching if you want to be a successful student. I've never had a teacher pull me off to the side and say, "Paul, you seem to be struggling a bit. How can I change what I'm doing to help you?" It's never happened. Nor should it! There's no way that a teacher can adjust to the learning style of every student in a classroom. While passionate teachers will try to engage all students, the student is still expected to adjust to the demands and style of the instructor. A student that fails to adjust will fall behind in class, receive poor grades, and experience a semester that seems to last for an eternity.

These two concepts hold true in a biblical context as well: when we as Christians learn from our teacher, we must adjust ourselves to his methods. Who is the teacher? Take a look at the verses below, paying close attention to the italicized words (emphasis mine):

- **"Peter remembered what Jesus had said to the tree on the previous day and exclaimed, 'Look, *Rabbi*! The fig tree you cursed has withered and died!' " (Mark 11:21 NLT)**

- **Nicodemus comes to Jesus by night and says, "*Rabbi*, we know that You have come from God as a *teacher*; for no one can do these signs that you do unless God is with him." (John 3:2)**

- **Jesus corrects his disciples by saying, "Don't let anyone call you '*Rabbi*,' for you have only one teacher, and all of you are equal as brothers and sisters." (Matt. 23:8 NLT)**

Here and elsewhere, Jesus is referred to as *rabbi*. At the time, the word's basic meaning was "my master," "great one," or "teacher." All of these terms would apply to Jesus, but "teacher" seems especially applicable based on the context. Overall, Jesus is referred to as *rabbi* or *teacher* twenty-nine times in the Gospels. The noun (teacher) and verb (teach) combined are used of Jesus some ninety times. Prior to his earthly ministry, Jesus was a carpenter. During his earthly ministry, Jesus was a rabbi or teacher. That role continues today, with Jesus Christ teaching and guiding believers.

If every teacher is different, and if you must adjust to your teacher's style, how well are you adapting to the style of our ultimate teacher Jesus Christ?

The implications of this question are huge. You cannot adjust to what you do not know, and what you do not know can make all the difference. Understanding and adjusting to Christ's teaching style can be the difference between enjoying a vibrant relationship with him and struggling through religious duties performed out of obligation. Let's take this idea a little further.

It's true that the Bible speaks of the Holy Spirit as our teacher, who guides us into all truth.[1] However, Jesus said that the Holy Spirit testifies about Christ himself.[2] So as God indwells every believer through his Spirit, the Holy Spirit directs every believer back to Christ. Practically, this principle works as follows:

- **If you want to know God, then get to know Christ.**[3]

- **If you want to understand God's character, then study the character of Christ.**

- **If you want to see truth embodied, then look no further than Christ. He is the way, the truth, and the life.**

Jesus is our example. As a disciple, we are following Christ and need to understand how he relates to his disciples. The Holy Spirit enables us to understand who Jesus is, what he taught, and how he desires to live through us. Why? Because in Christ, all the fullness of Deity dwells in bodily form, and in him you have been made complete.

Why is any of this conversation relevant? As a pastor, people share their frustrations with me all the time:

"I don't understand what God is trying to teach me."

"I wish God would write his will in the sky."

"I pray but nothing seems to happen."

"I know God is trying to teach me something but I have no idea what it is."

If Christ is the fullness of truth, is it possible that our confusion is linked to not understanding and adjusting to the teaching style of Christ? Is it possible that Christ's earthly way of teaching has eternal relevance for our ongoing relationships with God? Could it be that Christians are looking for the answers on Sunday morning, yet God is giving answers throughout the week? Could it be that God's plans would be clear if we just knew what we were listening for? What if God were saying, "I'm using these circumstances to teach you an amazing truth," and we're saying, "God, please remove these circumstances so I can get on with life?" How well do we know Jesus' teaching style?

For most Christians, it's not hard to understand God's heart on issues that are clearly spelled out in Scripture. However, if we want to pursue God in all areas of our lives, if we want to hear God in prayer and rely on him in everything we do, it is imperative that we know his teaching style and adjust to it.

This brings me to the impetus behind this book. The essence of *Eight Questions* is birthed out of an eight-year journey with God, trying to figure him out. I wanted to know what God was doing and what he wanted me to do. I had questions that God didn't seem to answer. I had concerns that seemed to fall on deaf ears. Intellectually, I knew God was there; emotionally, it felt as though God didn't care.

During those eight years, I often felt like Jacob wrestling with God at the river Jabbok. Like everyone who's ever struggled with God, I just wanted to understand. It didn't have to be the answer I was hoping for. My sincere prayer was, "God, just help me understand."

I wish I could say that I had an epiphany and was instantly synced with God. Instead, I discovered that God's methods of teaching today can be traced back to how Jesus taught while on earth.

The more I understood the style of my rabbi, the more I could see his lessons—and answers—all around me. I noticed that God often connected my circumstances with truths he was sharing in the Bible. He would bring people into my life that expressed desires similar to the ones he was giving me. My experiences and things that I was learning seemed random but now were coming together in incredible teaching moments. I found myself walking away from Scripture not always with the answer but rather with lingering questions that led me to answers later on.

God wants to do the same work in your life. As stated previously, *Eight Questions* will help you deepen your relationship with Christ, develop a listening ear for God's voice, discover areas where God is at work in your life, and discern the teaching style used by Christ with his disciples. Throughout the book, you will see one big truth come alive: Everything God desires to do in and through our lives, he will accomplish out of the overflow of our relationship with him. As our relationship with Christ strengthens, it is amazing how many answers we discover.

Through the use of Scripture, stories, practical insight, and even a little humor, this book will help you discover lessons that God is teaching all around you. In fact, you may even find that the questions in this book match some of the ongoing questions of your heart. My prayer is that each reader will rediscover the joy of knowing Christ, find some answers for the journey, and develop a greater passion to follow our rabbi.

The Teaching Style of Our Rabbi

Maybe you've experienced this same scenario. You're in college, and you're signing up for new classes. Most of your core classes are behind you, and now it's time to focus on the subjects related to your major. As you skim the listings, you are thrilled to discover that the premier professor in your field is offering a class in the exact time slot you need. This professor is phenomenal. He has pioneered much of this field. He has been published in numerous journals; he has written several books; and his knowledge is considered unparalleled.

As you read over the class description, it sounds perfect. You sign up for a class and anxiously wait for the new semester to begin.

The first day is finally here. You get to class early to ensure that you get a great seat. That's important! Last semester you had a horrible seat in a couple of classes—there was the big-headed guy who sat in front of you in physics; the cackling corner behind you in English Lit; and there was the dude with the musky aftershave in Biology 301. It was not a fun semester. As you take your seat, it seems relatively "weirdo" free. That's a good start. You smile to yourself.

The auditorium fills. The room hums with hushed tones and the beeps of computers being turned on. The professor arrives about eight minutes late but that is to be expected with genius.

He steps up on the platform, sets his well-worn bag on the desk, and without saying a word, he begins to write on the board. The auditorium is silent. Everyone scrambles for notepads and computers. Unfortunately, the handwriting is small and hard to read. You quickly find your glasses.

While filling the board with information, he begins his lecture. His voice is soft and monotone. He does this weird twitchy thing with his hand. It's very distracting. He seems to ramble through subjects. Some parts seem to have nothing to do with the lecture. With the exception of a few small glances, he never faces the class.

For the next two hours, you become painfully aware of a simple truth: how you teach is almost as important as what you say.

The topic could be amazing. The audience members could be on the edge of their seats. The teacher could be filled with insight. But if the presentation fails to connect, it all becomes noise.

How you teach is almost as important as what you say.

Take that concept and move it toward Christ. Jesus was a rabbi or teacher. Does the Bible reveal the teaching style of Jesus? People are far more familiar with what Jesus taught than how he taught it. That is to be expected, and in the broad scheme of things, it's better for people to remember "love your neighbor as yourself" than to know that Jesus used a common rabbinical technique while sharing it. However, as Christians cultivate intimate relationships with Christ, they need to see both what he said and how he said it.

> HOW YOU TEACH IS ALMOST AS IMPORTANT AS WHAT YOU SAY.

The more we understand his style, the more we will recognize his lessons all around us. It's not that God has been silent during the difficult times; the problem is that many Christians don't know what to listen for and, subsequently, miss so much of what he says.

What is the teaching style of Jesus? The New Testament gives us a number of clues. Mark tells us, "They were amazed at His teaching; for He was teaching them as one having authority, and not as the scribes."[1] We find an almost identical passage in the book of Matthew, just after Jesus delivered the Sermon on the Mount.[2] In these passages, we have our first clue. Jesus' style was authoritative. He was not speaking in possibilities, probabilities, or assumptions. He was not teaching as one unsure of his position. He did not need to emulate another well-known teacher to gain recognition. He taught with authority, and people recognized the authority as unusual.

A second clue can be found in Jesus' triumphal entry of Matthew 21. The story tells us that children shout, "Hosanna to the Son of David."[3] The chief priests and scribes are upset by this, and Jesus says, "Have you never read, 'Out of the mouth of infants and nursing babies you have prepared praise for Yourself'?"[4] The quote is originally found in Psalm 8:2. However, the statement shared by Jesus is not the whole statement. The original quote in Psalm 8:2 (NLT) goes on to say, "Silencing your enemies and all who oppose you." In this instance, Jesus was using a rabbinical teaching technique called *remez* (or hint). The teacher would share a portion of the text assuming the audience's knowledge of the Scriptures. He would then allow the audience members to finish the passage in their minds, thus deducing the meaning of the quote for themselves. In Matthew 21, the children and infants are praising God, and in so doing, they are silencing God's enemies. The implication is that the chief priests and scribes were God's enemies. Jesus used this technique constantly in the Gospels.

A third clue is found in the gospel of Mark. The passage says, "In [Jesus'] public ministry he never taught without using parables; but afterward, when he was alone with his disciples, he explained everything to them."[5] Matthew provides an almost identical passage.[6] Depending on which list you read, there are around fifty-seven universally recognized parables that Jesus taught. Altogether, there are more than 3,500 parables from first-century rabbis that are still in existence today, and Jesus' are considered some of the best. Based on these two texts, we find another valuable clue about Jesus' teaching style: in public, he never taught without using parables.

The use of parable is more significant than just telling a story as an illustration. The word *parable* comes from two words: the verb *ballō* (to throw, lay, or place) and the prefix *para* (alongside of). Together, the two words give the idea of placing or laying something alongside something else for the purpose of comparison.

Jesus would share an everyday story, and then he would lay a spiritual truth alongside it. It's an effective teaching technique because it enables listeners to take abstract concepts (for example, the kingdom of God, faith, forgiveness, heaven, and hell) and relate it to things they already know.

There's another reason that using parables is effective in teaching: a parable often requires focused thought from the listener. In Matthew 13, there are seven parables listed. Jesus gives parables about sowing and reaping, wheat and tares, mustard seed, leaven, treasure, pearls, and a dragnet. Most of these parables are just a few verses, but they force you to stop and think. The truth of a parable is rarely found on the surface; the listener must think through the story, the implications, the comparisons, and even the context to fully grasp the concept. By using parable, Jesus placed spiritual truths alongside everyday stories and encouraged listeners to really think about what was being shared.

A fourth clue about Jesus' teaching style can be seen in Matthew 6. Jesus says, "Look at the birds of the air, that they do not sow, nor reap nor gather into barns, and yet your heavenly Father feeds them. Are you not worth much more than they?"[7] In this passage, Jesus directs the listeners' attention to birds. In Matthew 22, Jesus said, "Show Me the coin used for the poll-tax ... Whose likeness and inscription is this? ... Render to Caesar the things that are Caesar's; and to God the things that are God's."[8] In the second passage, Jesus directs the people's attention to a coin. Here's the point: Jesus taught as he went, and he used examples that he found along the way. Throughout the Gospels, we see that Jesus used vineyards, brides, sheep, goats, refuse piles, leaven, bread, water, wells, neighbors, birds, foxes, and so many other examples in his teaching. He taught as he went and used examples along the way.

Finally, Jesus' teaching style incorporated the use of questions. This was not unique to Jesus; rather, it was a common rabbinical technique. Instead of giving all the answers to his students (and by-passing their need to think), the rabbi would guide his disciples to truth through a series of questions.

Here are just a few of the questions Jesus asked:

> **"Who are My mother and My brothers?"**[9]

> **"Who do people say that the Son of Man is?"**[10]

> **"Why are you asking Me about what is good?"**[11]

> **"Why are you afraid, you men of little faith?"**[12]

> **"Do you believe that I am able to do this?"**[13]

> **"Who of you by being worried can add a single hour to his life?"**[14]

> **"For who is greater, the one who reclines at the table
> or the one who serves?"**[15]

These clues give us a pretty good idea of Jesus' teaching style. While there were other techniques that were distinctly Jewish, the techniques mentioned give us a good place to begin. At this point, we can see how Jesus' earthly teaching style with his disciples correlates to our relationship with Christ today.

Jesus taught with authority, quoting portions of Scripture as he went, using everyday examples, sharing truth through stories, and constantly asking questions. Now that we have identified Jesus' teaching style, we can discern teachable moments in our lives. Jesus will teach you through Scripture. Therefore, it is imperative to spend time with God in his word. When he speaks through Scripture or prayer, you can recognize his voice as having authority. He will use everyday examples to get your attention. Folding laundry may seem "unspiritual," but Jesus can use the ordinary events of living to teach us about service, sacrifice, loving people, contentment, and so on. He will reveal great truths in everyday stories. A friend may share a story about the car breaking down and God supplying the money to fix it. That simple story can be used as a catalyst to teach us about faith and trusting God. Finally, he will pepper our minds with lingering questions.

It's these questions that have captured my attention. While all of these methods are represented in Jesus' teaching style, the use of questions weaves its way through each part.

When teaching authoritatively, he asked questions. When quoting portions of Scripture, he asked questions. When teaching parables, he asked questions. While teaching as he went, he asked questions. While using everyday examples, he asked questions. Jesus constantly asked questions.

It is the use of questions that is so foreign to how people in the West learn. In our society, we are programmed to think that the one who presents the problem is also the one who provides the answer. We don't like to wrestle with questions for too long. We like quick resolve. We want answers now.

This drive for immediate answers is one of the reasons people get upset with counseling. They want someone else to give them the answers, fix their problems, and let them get on with life. It's one of the reasons that people go to others for advice before really thinking through the problem. People run to friends, counselors, talk shows, pastors, teachers, or anyone else who may have an answer. We are not always concerned about learning the lesson; we simply want the answer.

We take the same approach with God. We are not always interested in the lessons God is teaching; our minds are fixated on finding answers to the problems we face. We want God to open our minds, remove the trash, instill the truth, close us back up, and let us be on our way.

We need to remember that God is focused on character transformation, not quick answers. He is moving us toward intimacy, not immediacy. God teaches us from the perspective of eternity, not a stopwatch.

If you and I want to learn what God is teaching, we need to let go of our obsession with time and start embracing the teaching style of Christ. He will teach with authority, quoting portions of Scripture as we go, using everyday examples, and constantly asking questions. Sometimes the teaching style of Jesus may seem like the ebb and flow of life. Your lessons for the day may be delivered in ten minutes of Bible reading, a child crying at your feet, a phone call from a hurting friend, and a great evening home with your family. It looks like normal life, but Jesus uses the temporal things to teach us the eternal. God may cause one verse from Scripture to stay in your mind for the day. The child crying at your feet can remind you of how we come before God (broken and in need of help). The phone call from a hurting friend may be God's invitation to die to self and serve others. A great evening home with your family may elicit prayers of thankfulness to God. Life is his classroom, but questions are his invitation.

Pay close attention to the little questions that appear throughout the day. Sometimes these questions seem as though your mind is just wandering. At other times, these questions stand out because they seem to come from nowhere. When a child is crying at your feet and you feel overwhelmed, God may ask a simple question, "Why are you upset?" As you think about the question, you may discover that you're upset because the crying is inconvenient. You had other plans. God's next question may be, "Is life about you?" Instantly, there is perspective you didn't have five minutes ago. God's questions are invitations for dialogue and discovery. Think about them, meditate upon them, and ask God to clarify them.

At this point, we've discussed Jesus' teaching style. We can see that he teaches as we go through life using ordinary situations, everyday stories, Scripture, authority, and questions. Begin to focus on these areas in your life. How is God using your daily routine as a classroom for character development? If we miss the daily lessons in order to focus on formalized teaching, we miss so much of what God is trying to share. There is no doubt that God shares biblical truth in worship services and Bible studies, but those are not God's only methods for teaching his people. What is God teaching through the normal ebb and flow of your life?

If you're having a hard time pinpointing specific lessons or major themes, begin to pay attention to the lingering questions. If a major part of Jesus' style is the use of questions, what is the rabbi asking you? What are the first questions that pop into your head when things go wrong? What are the recurring questions that you've wrestled with over the past six months to one year? Do not dismiss the questions as an overactive imagination. Sometimes, it's just you. But other times, it is God.

Each subsequent chapter shares a question Jesus asked me at moments in my life when I was trying to understand his lessons. My focus is on the questions. You will see that these questions are intertwined with everyday situations, truths through stories, authoritative teachings, and the use of Scripture. God used all of these to get my attention and plant recurring questions in my mind. I've found that the questions are God's invitation to join him in the process. It's by thinking through the questions, dialoguing with God, and following his gentle nudges that I've found answers.

I will warn you in advance. You may not get the answers you want. You may not like God's timing or his methods of delivery. However, it's in the process that you get to know him. Isn't that the goal anyway?

Take some time to reflect over what's been shared. The next eight chapters involve eight of the primary questions God has been asking me. Who knows—maybe he's asking you the same thing right now?

Personal Reflection/Group Discussion

1. What are some common themes that God is addressing in your life (for example, trust, loving people, prayer, and so on)? (You can recognize the themes because you tend to see them everywhere. God addresses this area in your devotional time, a friend brings up the same subject in a conversation, the pastor just preached on the subject last week, a book you're reading has an entire chapter dedicated to the same theme, and so forth.) The major themes of our lives are usually developed over months to years. Write down these themes.

_____

_____

_____

_____

_____

_____

2. Based on the teaching style of Jesus, how has he been trying to get your attention in these areas? Are lessons being taught through your children, your friends, work, church, Scripture, problems or crises, or blessings and answered prayers? Write some of the ordinary ways that God is teaching you right now.

_____

_____

_____

_____

_____

_____

_____

3. If you have not been able to discern the themes of your life or the ways that God is teaching, what can you do to recognize the teaching techniques of Jesus in your life? You know that he teaches through Scripture, with authority, as we go, using everyday examples, by sharing truth through stories, and by asking questions. Could the lack of focus indicate a lack of time spent reading the Bible, a lack of fellowship with the body, a lack of prayer, or a lack of time to reflect? What can you do to better recognize the teaching techniques of Christ?

_____

_____

_____

_____

_____

_____

_____

EIGHT QUESTIONS

...and the God who's asking.

1 A Relational Question

My wife and I have been married for fifteen years. We met in 1995 in the college-and-career class of the church we attended. In the months leading up to this fateful encounter, I was only attending worship services at the church. One day my dad said, "Paul, if you ever want to get married, you need to go to Sunday school." For most people, that comment sounds like something a Christian dad would tell his Christian son. But you need to know something about my dad. He doesn't talk much. He's quiet! In fact, this could be the only dating advice he ever gave me. Needless to say, when the advice was offered, I listened.

The following week, I went to Sunday school, and the first person to greet me at the door was Brea. We went from meeting to married in eleven months. I know it sounds fast, but we both knew what we were looking for in a spouse. We talked about the importance of our walk with God, the potential for a life in ministry, raising kids, personal goals, family values, finances, and communication. We left no rock unturned.

There was something else we talked about while dating—divorce. It may sound strange to discuss divorce before getting married, but that subject was very important to both of us. We each held the conviction that divorce was not an option, and the other person needed to know that before saying, "I do."

Our conviction about divorce has shaped the way we go through the difficult times. Like every other couple, we have arguments and disagreements. We don't always see eye to eye. However, regardless of the argument, the subject of divorce never comes up. Divorce is not an option in our home.

Those early conversations gave us a framework for understanding this principle: knowing your options before the trials will narrow your focus through the trials.

In this chapter, I want to help people narrow down some options. There is no doubt that God will allow you to go through things that will challenge your faith and leave you with more questions than answers. Problems and trials are a part of life. When those times come, how will you respond to God?

When God doesn't make sense, circumstances are overwhelming, and your spiritual life is on the rocks, what will you do? When the Bible is hard to understand, your prayers seem unanswered, and you don't recognize God's work in your life, how will you respond? When you have more questions than answers and more problems than solutions, do you have a predetermined course of action? If you have never taken the "quit" option off the table, you may not have the determination to embrace the concepts of this chapter. This chapter involves the relentless pursuit of Christ. It encourages Christians to choose this pursuit before encountering the trial. When you have clear direction for your life, it enables you to press on while encountering the temporary fog of circumstances. Will we choose to follow Christ in intimate relationship no matter what happens? Knowing your options before the trials will narrow your focus through the trials.

> KNOWING YOUR OPTIONS BEFORE THE TRIALS WILL NARROW YOUR FOCUS THROUGH THE TRIALS.

To express this concept through Scripture, let's move through a familiar story. When we get to the end of the story, I'll share one relational question that needs to be answered *today*. This question is between you and God. This question cannot wait. As you read through the story, take note of the italicized portions (emphasis mine). Each of these sections corresponds to a teaching technique of Christ. In these first couple of chapters, I will take the time to emphasize the techniques. The more we recognize the teaching style of Jesus, the easier it will be to recognize God's lessons and answers in our lives. The story is found in Mark 8:27–38:

Jesus went out, along with *His disciples*, to the villages of Caesarea Philippi; and *on the way He questioned His disciples, saying to them, "Who do people say that I am?"* They told Him, saying, "John the Baptist; and others say Elijah; but others, one of the prophets." *And He continued by questioning them, "But who do you say that I am?"* Peter answered and said to Him, "You are the Christ." And He warned them to tell no one about Him.

And *He began to teach them* that the Son of Man must suffer many things and be rejected by the elders and the chief priests and the scribes, and be killed, and after three days rise again. *And He was stating the matter plainly.* And Peter took Him aside and began to rebuke Him. But turning around and seeing His disciples, He rebuked Peter and said, "Get behind Me, Satan; for you are not setting your mind on God's interests, but man's."

And He summoned the crowd with His disciples, and said to them, "If anyone wishes to come after Me, he must deny himself, and take up his cross and follow Me. For whoever wishes to save his life will lose it, but whoever loses his life for My sake and the gospel's will save it. *For what does it profit a man to gain the whole world, and forfeit his soul? For what will a man give in exchange for his soul?* For whoever is ashamed of Me and My words in this adulterous and sinful generation, the Son of Man will also be ashamed of him when He comes in the glory of His Father with the holy angels."

Notice that Jesus taught his disciples "on the way." Then after asking two questions, "He began to teach them." Jesus didn't wait until they were in the synagogue. He didn't pause for them to pull out notebooks and record the lesson. He taught as he went. The text also says that he "questioned His disciples" and "He continued by questioning them." There are four very important questions that Jesus asked his disciples. The first two deal with his identity; the second two deal with our soul.

Verse 32 says, "And He was stating the matter plainly." I love this statement. Not only can we see the authoritative style of Jesus' teaching, but there is another lesson that is extremely personal. I've often told God, "If you will just make your will plain, I'll do it. God, speak clearly. God, make it so understandable that I can't mess it up. If you do that, I will get it done!" Somehow I've convinced myself that the problem of communication is on God's side. If God would make his will plain, then I would get it. Since I'm not getting it, then obviously God is at fault.

In this text, Jesus made it plain, but the disciples still did not get it. "And Peter took Him aside and began to rebuke Him. But turning around and seeing His disciples, He rebuked Peter and said, 'Get behind Me, Satan; for you are not setting your mind on God's interests, but man's.'"[1]

The reason Jesus was going to be rejected, killed, and raised again was to accomplish the interests of God. God was in the process of reconciling humanity to himself. Peter got upset because he was focused on man's interests. If Jesus dies, what happens to his future? You can almost hear the arguments of Peter: "Hey, Jesus, we've followed you for three years, and this was not a part of our plan. Our plan is to be with you when you establish your kingdom on earth. We want a place at the table. Besides, do you really want to be rejected and killed?" Peter is setting his mind on man's interest.

To show the stark contrast between God's interest and man's, Jesus calls the crowds and disciples together for a quick lesson. The lesson is found in verses 34–38:

> And He summoned the crowd with His disciples, and said to them, "If anyone wishes to come after Me, he must deny himself, and take up his cross and follow Me. For whoever wishes to save his life will lose it, but whoever loses his life for My sake and the gospel's will save it. For what does it profit a man to gain the whole world, and forfeit his soul? For what will a man give in exchange for his soul? For whoever is ashamed of Me and My words in this adulterous and sinful generation, the Son of Man will also be ashamed of him when He comes in the glory of His Father with the holy angels."

While it's important to grasp the lesson, I also want you to see the format:

Verse 34 is a statement.

Verse 35 is a statement.

Verse 36 is a question.

Verse 37 is a question.

Verse 38 is a statement.

There are three statements and two questions. Do you know what you do not see? A single answer!

The questions of Christ will cause us to think. He asks questions that disturb our consciences and make us ask questions of ourselves. After reading these verses, I find myself asking a number of difficult questions:

Am I willing to deny myself to follow Christ?

Am I trying to save my life or lose it?

What would I give in exchange for my soul?

Am I ashamed of Christ and his words?

Will the Son of Man be ashamed of me?

Jesus didn't need to teach for forty-five minutes to get a point across. He gave three statements and two questions that could be summarized in one minute, and he left people with more than they could say grace over.

I have two reasons for showing you this text. First, I want you to see Jesus' teaching style in operation. Several of his techniques are clearly seen in this text. I pray that you will begin to identify his style and adjust to that style.

The second reason I share this text is to highlight a question that God has asked me hundreds of times in the past eight years. He could have been asking me the same question for most of my Christian life, but I never heard him because I didn't understand his style. There is a very good chance that he is asking you the same question. It's a relational question that may be stated in different ways, but the essence is the same.

> ## WILL YOU PURSUE ME IN THE PROCESS OF WHATEVER YOU ARE GOING THROUGH?

Jesus said in verse 34, "If anyone wishes to come after Me [not my blessings, not my answers, not my quick interventions, but Me], he must deny himself, and take up his cross and follow Me."

I can't tell you how many times I've begged God to change my circumstances, intervene on my behalf, or answer my prayers. Instead of giving an answer, God softly asks this question: "Paul, will you pursue me in the process of whatever you are going through?" God knows when you are hurting, confused, and tired. He also knows that our greatest need is not money, success, or an instant answer. Our greatest need is him.

Over the years, God has asked this question at key moments in my life. During my early years as a church planter, for instance.

In 2004, when we first started Life Baptist Church in Las Vegas, Nevada, we immediately ran into obstacles. For starters, some of our church planting support fell through. We were in a new city, with several families on payroll, and we found ourselves scrambling to make up a $40,000 deficit. I went to God. I asked him to send more partners, more people, and more support. Nothing seemed to happen. We sent support letters to every church we knew. We received no response. We shared the need with our core group. We prayed together and brought this financial burden before God. At times, it felt like no one heard our prayers. But after praying, a nagging question would come to mind: "Will you pursue me in the process of whatever you are going through?"

Space became the next obstacle. After the first several months of meeting in our home, our new church was averaging forty-five people. My daughters' rooms were set aside for childcare. The kitchen was the fellowship hall. Our living and dining rooms were set aside for worship. We set up chairs in open spaces and had people sitting on the staircase and in adjoining rooms. On one night, we had seventy-seven people piled into our little house.

We knew that we needed to find a public meeting space. Over the next several months, we asked twenty-nine schools on our side of town if they could host us. All twenty-nine schools said no. We went back to some of those schools a second time, and they still said no. We went to one school a third time, and they continued to say no. We looked for space in strip malls, warehouses, community clubhouses, and professional buildings. All of them said no.

It wasn't as though we were asking God to upgrade our meeting place from workable to desirable. We were praying for doable. We didn't have enough room for everyone to gather. The need was real. As a group, we prayed. For almost five months, nothing happened. However, all along the way, I continued to hear this question ringing in my ears: "Will you pursue me in the process of whatever you are going through?" The question didn't seem to make sense. I was asking God for a meeting place; he was asking me about an intimate relationship.

Then there was the issue of transiency. From August 2003 through June 2004, a number of families moved across the country to help us start the church. The moves were not easy. Within the first year, some of these families lost jobs, others couldn't find jobs, some got homesick, and some were going through personal issues. One by one, they began to move back to the South. There was a part of me that felt abandoned. I felt betrayed by God. It seemed as if God had moved us across the country and then left us. There was a part of me that felt responsible as a pastor. "If I would have been a better pastor or leader, they would have stayed." I begged God to help me understand his purpose in all of these things. I begged God to take away the feelings of emptiness and pain. In the silence, one question continued to race through my brain: "Will you pursue me in the process of whatever you are going through?"

Finally, whatever we did, it didn't seem as if the church was growing as it should. As the core group formed, we had mission teams come to Las Vegas to help us prayer walk neighborhoods, pass out flyers, host block parties, and serve people in the community. In the first two years, we prayer walked over 150,000 homes. We dropped off more than 200,000 invitations for ten to twelve events. We put out almost 150 road signs, sent invitations to more than 1,000,000 e-mail addresses, and served breakfast to thousands of motorists. Based on the saturation of material, the frequency of drops, and the principles of marketing, we were expecting 500 to 700 people to show up at church. It never happened.

Regardless of our efforts, we would see a minimal response. I would go back to my prayer closet and beg God for answers. What are we doing wrong? Where are the people? Have I missed your calling to start this church? God, where are you? And here's what I would hear: "Paul, will you pursue me in the process of whatever you are going through?"

After losing support, doors closing, families moving, and difficulty gathering a core group, I didn't know if I could take any more disappointment. God thought otherwise.

About that time, my wife noticed a couple of irregular spots on my back. I went to the doctor, who did a biopsy. A week later, they brought me back to the office and said, "You have a number of areas with pre-cancerous cells. These cells are beginning to advance, and we need to remove them immediately." On the first visit, they removed seven areas the size of a dime and froze thirty-two other places that were beginning to advance. I walked out of the office looking like a victim caught in a drive-by shooting.

I went into my prayer closet dumbfounded. "God, what else? What are you doing? I've got an infant and a toddler at home. We're in a new ministry. Our family is on the other side of the country. I'm discouraged, I'm tired, and I don't know how much more I can handle." Guess what I heard. "Will you pursue me in the process of whatever you are going through?"

Why have I shared all of these stories? Because I want you to know that if you are struggling to understand God and his purposes, I understand.

If you've begged God for an answer or wrestled with why God allows things to happen, I know how you feel. It's hard. It hurts. Sometimes it feels like God is nowhere to be found. But please listen to what I discovered!

I needed to answer God's question before I was prepared for him to answer mine.

I was asking for things; he was offering himself. I wanted blessings from God; he wanted to be my blessing. Like a child, I was trying to get the toy hidden behind my father's back; like a father, he was trying to get me to run into his arms.

After being worn down by the process, I began to pray Scripture back to God. I would say, "God, I do want to come after you; I am willing to deny myself; I am willing to take up my cross and follow you. God, I will pursue you. If you've not given an answer, it's because I'm not prepared to receive it. So God, do whatever it takes to get me ready. I'm coming after you."

You might be wondering, "Did everything change? Did God send more people? Did the $40,000 miraculously arrive? Did people stop moving away?" The short answer is no. God was not making a Hallmark movie; he was preparing me for a life of abiding in Christ. There was no fire from heaven or earth-shattering God-moment. But I will tell you what changed.

> I NEEDED TO ANSWER GOD'S QUESTION BEFORE I WAS PREPARED FOR HIM TO ANSWER MINE.

God changed my perspective on what I really needed. My first priority was not the church; it was to pursue Christ relationally. He became my pursuit. My greatest concern was no longer fulfilling my vision for the church but being a part of his. I spent a couple of years trying to find traction in this new life. People would say, "What's the vision of Life?" I would say, "I have no idea. I thought I knew when we started, but God changed all that. Until God clearly shows us his vision, we're just going to love God, love people, and make disciples." It's kind of funny when I think about it. Who knew that out of confusion God could bring focus?

I want to be quick to say that God has not kept us completely in the dark. In the past three or four years, God has blown us away with the careful and loving way he has formed Life Baptist Church. We've seen unbelievable resources come in. We've seen so many people saved and baptized. We've seen disciples made and sent. All of that has been great. But guess what has never changed? Pursing Christ is still my goal personally and our goal corporately.

Those who attend our church and listen to our messages online have asked me, "Why do you speak about relationship with Christ in almost every message?" My answer is simple. For over eight years, my rabbi has asked me one question through all the ups and downs of life: "Will you pursue me in the process of whatever you are going through?" When he stops emphasizing the importance of relationship, I will stop sharing it in every message.

Today, you may be able to relate to what I've been describing. You may be in several situations that seem to require God's immediate assistance, and he may seem silent. There is a possibility that you have also heard that faint call to pursue him. The words do not need to be the same, but the essence of the question will be. Will you pursue him? When you don't understand, will you follow after him? When the circumstances get worse, will you chase after him? When nothing goes right and you are mad at God, will you still follow after him? Knowing your options before the trials will narrow your focus through the trails.

This may be the first time you've ever considered that Jesus' style of teaching and your style of learning may clash. Maybe you've heard a similar question for years, but you didn't know how to define it or what to do with it. I leave you with the same question God has left with me. Will you pursue Christ in the process of whatever you are going through?

Personal Reflection/Group Discussion

1. What are you going through today that seems to take your focus away from pursuing Christ?

_____

_____

_____

_____

_____

_____

_____

_____

2. Why is it important to pursue Christ instead of answers to prayer?

_____

_____

_____

_____

_____

3. What are some different variations of the relational question? List different ways that God has called you to pursue him. What seems to be his favorite appeal in your life?

_____

_____

_____

_____

_____

4. How can you practically pursue Christ? What does that look like from day to day?

_____

_____

_____

_____

_____

2 A Faith Question

If you were to ask twenty different Christians what God is teaching them, I'm convinced that at least half would say that he's teaching them about faith. The other half would probably say that he's teaching them patience. Ironically, the second reply is what people say when God forces them to live by the first. While my statistics are somewhat facetious, the point is not. God is in the habit of teaching his people to live by faith.

Let's back up and review some critical information that we learned earlier in the book. The focus of *Eight Questions* is to help Christians understand God's teaching techniques and pinpoint the ways he speaks into our lives.

We opened the discussion with two general concepts:

1. **Every teacher is different.**

2. **You must adjust to their styles of teaching to be a successful student.**

These are important concepts to know because throughout Jesus' earthly ministry, he was referred to as *rabbi* or *teacher*. To this day, Jesus' followers are called *disciples*. He is our rabbi; we are his disciples.

Because of this teacher-student relationship, much of our lives will be spent in learning mode. God teaches us about himself, his desires, what it means to walk in relationship with him, what it means to love others, and what it means to serve and give ourselves to his kingdom agenda.

God is not limited to classroom discussions or book knowledge. Instead, he uses the Bible, the church, circumstances, tragedies, family and friends, marriage and children, finances, obstacles, accomplishments, experiences, and so many other things to teach us. God combines everyday examples, authoritative teachings in Scripture, individual stories, and a barrage of questions to lead us to truth. It's a process. If we do not understand how God uses the "ordinary" to teach us, we can miss so much of what God is sharing.

The focus of this chapter is a single question of faith. The exact wording of the question may be different as God asks us individually, but the essence of what he's asking us will be the same.

I think God asks this question so often that you may think it is just your conscience speaking to you. You will hear God ask this question when you're going through trials and you don't know what to do. You will hear God whisper this question into your heart when you're facing financial concerns and it seems like your options are out. God will ask this question when you're in hospital rooms, leaving job interviews, and wrestling with deep truths. It seems to be a common question that he asks when the circumstances you face require grace, forgiveness, or patience.

The question God asks at so many pivotal points in your life is:

"WILL YOU TRUST ME?"

Let's explore this question together, starting from Hebrews 11:1–13:

> Now faith is the assurance of things hoped for, the conviction of things not seen. For by it the men of old gained approval.
>
> By faith we understand that the worlds were prepared by the word of God, so that what is seen was not made out of things which are visible.
>
> By faith Abel offered to God a better sacrifice than Cain, through which he obtained the testimony that he was righteous, God testifying about his gifts, and through faith, though he is dead, he still speaks.

By faith Enoch was taken up so that he would not see death; and he was not found because God took him up; for he obtained the witness that before his being taken up he was pleasing to God. And without faith it is impossible to please Him, for he who comes to God must believe that He is and that He is a rewarder of those who seek Him.

By faith Noah, being warned by God about things not yet seen, in reverence prepared an ark for the salvation of his household, by which he condemned the world, and became an heir of the righteousness which is according to faith.

By faith Abraham, when he was called, obeyed by going out to a place which he was to receive for an inheritance; and he went out, not knowing where he was going. By faith he lived as an alien in the land of promise, as in a foreign land, dwelling in tents with Isaac and Jacob, fellow heirs of the same promise; for he was looking for the city which has foundations, whose architect and builder is God.

By faith even Sarah herself received ability to conceive, even beyond the proper time of life, since she considered Him faithful who had promised. Therefore there was born even of one man, and him as good as dead at that, as many descendants as the stars of heaven in number, and innumerable as the sand which is by the seashore.

All these died in faith, without receiving the promises, but having seen them and having welcomed them from a distance, and having confessed that they were strangers and exiles on the earth.

We could literally open our Bibles at random and point to a verse, and there's a good chance that we would hit a story regarding faith. Notable examples include…

- **when Abraham was asked to sacrifice Isaac** [1];

- **when Joshua was instructed to march around Jericho** [2];

- **when Daniel faced the lion's den** [3];

- **when the disciples were told to leave everything and follow Christ** [4]; **and**

- **when the centurion begged Christ to heal his servant** [5].

In all of these stories, God asks the same question: "Will you trust me?" The stories change, but the question remains the same.

The Bible is filled with faith stories, but it would be impractical to cover each story in detail. Hebrews 11 is beneficial because the entire chapter is dedicated to faith, and it gives a recap of numerous faith stories. There is another reason that Hebrews 11 is so crucial to the discussion of faith: it shows that the outcome of great faith is not always the answer we want.

Before we go any further, I have a question for you. How is God challenging your faith today? Are there situations in your life right now where you can hear God ask the question, "Will you trust me?" The question may seem small, but its importance is difficult to adequately describe. (Take a moment to turn to the Personal Reflection/Group Discussion section at the end of this chapter, and list the ways God is currently challenging your faith.)

> THE OUTCOME OF GREAT FAITH IS NOT ALWAYS THE ANSWER WE WANT.

Why is the faith question so important? First, it challenges us to define where we are placing our faith. "Will you trust *me*?" It's not uncommon for Christians to replace "me" with something else, such as a desired outcome, a misunderstood promise, a passage taken out of context, or bad advice.

For example, let's say you're interviewing for a job that you really want. On the morning of the interview, you come across Jeremiah 29:11 (NIV): " 'For I know the plans I have for you,' declares the Lord, 'plans to prosper you and not to harm you; plans to give you hope and a future.' " You're excited about the passage, and you share it with a Christian friend because you feel that God has given you a word for the day. Your friend says, "That's a sign from God. He is going to give you that job." It seems to make sense. You want the job, you have a passage from the Bible, and a Christian friend is in agreement, so you take that as a promise from God. God has declared it! You're going to get the job.

The interview is great. You knock it out of the park, and it only confirms your belief that God has promised you this job. Later that day, the company calls you back and says, "Thank you for interviewing, but we've decided to go with someone else." You're shocked. You may even get upset with God. "Hey, God, you promised! What about that passage and your plan for me? What about my friend being in agreement? This job seemed perfect. Why did you let me down?"

Did God let you down? No. Here are just a handful of reasons to support that answer: (1.) Jeremiah was giving a promise to the nation of Israel—not a New Testament believer. (2.) There is a difference between Christian advice and godly counsel. Christians are often wrong. Godly counsel is insight based on God's truth. (3.) What you want might not be what you need. Could it be that God is protecting you from some unforeseen issue down the road? (4.) Christians have a tendency to read God's promises into our circumstances when it's advantageous. We're not quite as quick to embrace other promises from Scripture:

- **"Be sure your sin will find you out."** [6]

- **"You cannot serve God and wealth."** [7]

- **"In the world you have tribulation, but take courage;
  I have overcome the world."** [8]

- **"But even if you should suffer for the sake of righteousness,
  you are blessed."** [9]

Those are promises from Scripture as well, but they can be a bit cumbersome when we're trying to get our own way.

When God asks us if we will trust him, he is bringing our attention back to the source of our faith. Is my faith in a passage that may or may not be in context? Is my faith in a desired outcome or in the well-meaning counsel of a friend? Is my faith in what I would do if I were God? Or is my faith *in* God?

Second, it challenges us to answer the question personally. "Will *you* trust me?" It's not uncommon for Christians to replace *you* with *they*.

We as Christians have an amazing tendency to justify our position before God. "God, my parents have been Christians for years, and they say this is right. My pastor preached on this topic last week so I guess it's true. My spouse seems to get results when he or she prays so here I am."

We do not get to live vicariously through the faith of others. There is going to be a day when it is just you and God. Your parents are not around; your pastor is not around; and your friends are not around. It's just you and God, and the question God will ask is "Will *you* trust me?"

Third, it challenges us to acknowledge our dependence upon God. "Will you *trust* me?" People are taught to be self-reliant, and trusting others does not come easily.

We have been conditioned by society to rise to the challenge, take the bull by the horns, and get things done. The world praises self-made people. We lift them up as heroes who have been able to take on the adversity of the world with strong will, determination, discipline, and hard work. Self-reliance is considered a virtue by our society.

I need to be careful to point out that relying on Christ *is not* the same as doing nothing. Relying on Christ means that we act after he directs, in the way that he directs, and through the enabling he provides. We're still *doing* things; it just flows out of *being* with him.

When God asks us to trust him, it is a reminder to ask ourselves in turn, "Will I trust in God, or will I trust in myself?"

Let's jump back into the text now. As we go through it, I want you to take note of the different situations, the different outcomes, and the same basic question. Hebrews 11:1–2 reads, "Now faith is the assurance of things hoped for, the conviction of things not seen. For by it the men of old gained approval."

We get a simple definition of faith and a primary reason that faith is a part of our lives. Faith is defined by two words in verse 1: assurance and conviction (not wishes and want-to's, not maybe's and could-be's, but assurance and conviction).

How often do we have complete assurance or total conviction about any circumstance? It's rare, if ever! But as Christians, we can have assurance and conviction in God and in his word. We can be confident in who God is and what God said. By definition alone, faith should guide us back to God. This concept forms the basis of faith.

"For by it the men of old gained approval." When people exercise faith in God, he is pleased. Why? Verse 6 tells us. "Without faith it is impossible to please Him, for he who comes to God must believe that He is." Stop right there! He must believe that God is *what*? Is there! We must believe that God is there, that God exists. We must believe that God is not a figment of our imagination. The person who comes to God must first believe that he is there, and that he is a rewarder of those who seek him.

Hebrews 11:3–12 gives some examples and stories of people living by faith. Let's begin in verse 3: "By faith we understand that the worlds were prepared by the word of God, so that what is seen was not made out of things which are visible."

This statement is about creation, God's power, and God's word. "By faith we understand." Said in a different way, "Without faith, you will never understand." It's pretty easy! Either God lied in the book of Genesis, or he told the truth. If he told the truth, then he is all-powerful because he created everything out of nothing by the power of his word. If he told the truth, then he is trustworthy because his word is true.

Someone may ask, "How can you be sure that God had anything to do with creation?" The answer for a Christian living by faith is because God clearly and authoritatively declared it in the Bible. In deep matters of creation and science, God has a question for you: "Will you trust me?" By faith, you understand.

Our next faith story in Hebrews 11:4 speaks of the first two siblings of Scripture: "By faith Abel offered to God a better sacrifice than Cain, through which he obtained the testimony that he was righteous, God testifying about his gifts, and through faith, though he is dead, he still speaks."

In this story, Cain and Abel brought a sacrifice to God. Somewhere along the way, God instructed them in the proper ways of worship. There must have been previous instructions because they came to the proper place, they came at the appointed time, and they both brought an offering. Cain was a farmer and brought the fruit of the ground. Abel was a hunter and brought a blood sacrifice. God accepted Abel's sacrifice and he rejected Cain's.

Cain got mad and killed his brother. Don't let the bluntness of that statement pass you by. Cain got mad *and killed his brother*. Wait a minute! That's not how a faith story is supposed to go. If Abel showed up at the right place, at the right time, and with the right offering—doing everything God required—why did he get killed?

That doesn't make sense. Abel is the good guy, and he's dead. Cain is the bad guy, and he's living. You might think that the person who puts their faith in God is always going to have a happy ending. They are always going to get what they want. But that's not a biblical concept of faith. In difficult matters of loss and grief, God is still asking, "Will you trust me?"

Hebrews 11:5–6 tells of a man named Enoch who never saw death:

> By faith Enoch was taken up so that he would not see death; and he was not found because God took him up; for he obtained the witness that before his being taken up he was pleasing to God. And without faith it is impossible to please Him, for he who comes to God must believe that He is and that He is a rewarder of those who seek Him.

There are two people in the Bible that never faced death: Enoch and Elijah. Both guys were taken by God in a supernatural way. There is not much information on Enoch, but what we do have is found in Genesis:

> Enoch lived sixty-five years, and became the father of Methuselah. Then Enoch walked with God three hundred years after he became the father of

Methuselah, and he had other sons and daughters. So all the days of Enoch were three hundred and sixty-five years. Enoch walked with God; and he was not, for God took him.[10]

What does it mean, "God took him"? People don't just disappear. Are we supposed to believe that on this day Enoch is hanging out minding his own business and the next moment he's in eternity? The entire story is strange. It doesn't make sense. I think that's the point God is making. In matters that you don't understand and you cannot explain, God is still asking, "Will you trust me?"

This next story is probably one of the most famous Bible stories. We find the story of Noah in Hebrews 11:7:

By faith Noah, being warned by God about things not yet seen, in reverence prepared an ark for the salvation of his household, by which he condemned the world, and became an heir of the righteousness which is according to faith.

Most people know this story. The world was incredibly wicked, so God chose to destroy the world, but he identified Noah and his family as righteous. He told Noah to build an ark. It took 120 years from the time Noah started building the ark for the floodwaters to come.

One hundred and twenty years is a long time to do something that makes sense, much less to do something that seems crazy. Do you know how much faith it would take to cut down that first tree? Do you know how much faith it would take to keep working while you were rapidly becoming the neighborhood lunatic?

Has God ever asked you to do something that you don't fully understand? Has that task or that step of obedience continued to go on and on? Even though you don't know all the details, God is asking, "Will you trust me?"

Next we find Abraham's story, as shared in Hebrews 11:8–12. It includes a few major steps of faith:

By faith Abraham, when he was called, obeyed by going out to a place which he was to receive for an inheritance; and he went out, not knowing where he was going. By faith he lived as an alien in the land of promise, as in a foreign land, dwelling in tents with Isaac and Jacob, fellow heirs of the same promise; for he was looking for the city which has foundations, whose architect and builder is God.

By faith even Sarah herself received ability to conceive, even beyond the proper time of life, since she considered Him faithful who had promised. Therefore there was born even of one man, and him as good as dead at that, as many descendants as the stars of heaven in number, and innumerable as the sand which is by the seashore.

These verses describe the life of Abraham and Sarah, highlighting two big "faith" moments in their lives. The first moment was when God came to Abraham and told him to pack up and move. God didn't tell him where he was going but he obeyed anyway.

The second faith moment occurred when Abraham and Sarah were promised a son. Not only were they going to have a son, but their descendants would be as numerous as the stars of the sky.[11] When the promise came, Abraham was seventy-five years old and Sarah was sixty-five years old.[12] When Isaac (their promised son) arrived, Abraham was one hundred years old and Sarah was ninety years old.[13] Twenty-five years passed between the initial promise and the fulfillment of that promise.

This story has so many faith components. It's a crazy story if you factor in their ages alone. It's even crazier when you realize that Sarah was barren.[14] And it wasn't as though they were trying to have their tenth child at such a late age. This was the first child!

Both stories help us see the same truth. It doesn't matter if God calls you to do something and doesn't give you the details, or if God promises that he'll do something that seems impossible. His question for you will be the same: "Will you trust me?"

When we put all of these stories together, we can hear God asking,

"In deep matters of creation and science, will you trust me?"

"In difficult matters of loss and grief, will you trust me?"

"In matters you don't understand and can't explain, will you trust me?"

"In huge challenges that require great patience, will you trust me?"

"When I call you to do something without giving you the details, will you trust me?"

"If I promise that I'll do something that seems absolutely impossible, will you trust me?"

The situations change, but the question remains the same.

Why do we need to answer this question? Hebrews 11:13 helps put everything into perspective: "All these died in faith, without receiving the promises, but having seen them and having welcomed them from a distance, and having confessed that they were strangers and exiles on the earth."

God asks the question because sometimes you don't get to see the completed picture. You may never understand all of his reasons on this side of heaven. There are promises that God keeps in time, and there are promises God keeps in eternity. You might be on the front side of a one-hundred-year promise, and God takes you home at year ten. God may allow you to see steps 1–3 but not steps 4–10. Are you okay with that? Are you willing to relinquish the immediate need for answers to respond positively to God's question, "Will you trust me?"

We all can look back and see moments when God has asked us to do exactly that. Sometimes the question comes before the answer. Sometimes the question comes with the answer. Sometimes the question is all you get.

When we started the church in Las Vegas, one of the families that moved here to help was the Heltons. They had a little girl named Gracie who had a brain tumor. For a couple of years prior to relocating, they sensed God prompting them to move to the west coast and be a part of a church plant. They didn't know all the details, but like Abram, they packed up everything and moved west. They got settled into the city, and things seemed to be going great. They were active in the church, they made a lot of friends, and they could see God provide in so many ways. But they encountered a huge problem.

The medication Gracie needed for pain was not covered by insurance in the state of Nevada. They filled out paperwork requesting Medicare coverage instead. We prayed as a church that the request would be approved, but it was denied. If they had to pay out of pocket, it would cost several thousand dollars a month. There was no way they could sustain those bills. They were faced with the difficult question of staying in Las Vegas or moving back to their hometown so they could afford their daughter's care.

The answer was both simple and hard. The first responsibility of all parents is to care for their children, but it didn't make leaving the city and the church any easier. They were now wrestling with a different set of questions. "God, why did you move us across the country? God, why didn't the paperwork go through? Are we not trusting you by going home?" These are questions to which we may never know the answer. But God's question was still the same: "Will you trust me?"

Our circumstances don't need to make sense. God doesn't need to respond in a way that eases our minds or connects the dots. The story doesn't need a fairy-tale ending. For that matter, the story doesn't need to fit nicely into our theological expectations. The question is still the same: "Will you trust me?"

The church's trust in God was tested again on April 29, 2003. I was anxious about the amount of money we needed to start Life Baptist. God was bringing in resources but not as quickly as I had hoped. Granted, the week before April 29, God provided $75,000 in support funds. But that was last week! This week, I struggled to see where the other funds would come from. Have you ever noticed that we have spiritual amnesia when we're facing a new challenge? We forget what God just did on our behalf. Anyway, I was anxious and worried, but that morning I was reading in Psalm 37. Verse 34 (NLT) says, "Don't be impatient for the Lord to act! Travel steadily along his path."

In my journal, I wrote, "Thank you, Lord, for the reminder. I can trust in you."

In my mind, it seemed as though this verse was assurance that the money was coming soon, a reminder to help me hold on to hope just a little bit longer. But the money didn't come. Instead of providing the funds we thought we needed, God helped us find cheaper insurance, cheaper office space, and better ways to be stewards of his resources. For over a year, we had no idea how the bills were going to be paid.

Instead of sending us a check, God sent us a value. He taught us the value of God-dependence! All the while, he kept asking, "Will you trust me?"

In the summer of 2004, two of our college students were preparing to go to Poland on a mission trip. For months, they prayed, prepared, sent support letters, and did everything they could to get the money they needed.

One Sunday before service, they both came to me very upset. They didn't understand why God had not answered their prayers. They needed to have their money within a couple of weeks, and they were not even close. I didn't have anything profound to share, but my comment was, "If God wants you to go, he will make a way!"

After the morning service, they both came running back up to me. They said, "Did you hear about the check?" I hadn't heard anything. They went on to tell me that when the offering was counted, there was a check for $10,000. On the outside of the envelope was the note, "Please use this for missions." I was told later that the man who gave the check was passing through Las Vegas, heard about a church meeting in a casino, and decided to drop in and worship. We haven't seen him since.

To this day, both Andy and Sara remember God's incredible provision. They were able to see God tangibly answer their prayers in a matter of moments.

Here's my point. All Christians will encounter challenges to their faith. All of us will be put in situations that we cannot control, we cannot contain, and we cannot change. When you're in those situations, listen for God's question: "Will you trust me?" The question may come during the problem, it may come with the answer, or it may come in place of the answer. Will you trust God?

When you say yes, do not make the mistake of thinking that everything will turn out the way you hoped. Saying yes to the question is not a guarantee that you get the results you want. Saying yes to the question is a guarantee that you're on the right path for God's best.

So let me ask you several questions regarding faith. What crazy thing has God placed before you? What impossible situation are you facing? What challenge seems insurmountable? What opportunity is sitting just outside your reach where the only thing God seems to say is "Will you trust me?"

Do whatever God directs you to do, and once you have done it, wait. Allow the question to open dialogue between you and God. If you feel like you've been let down before, ask God what it means to trust him. Ask God to show you what you didn't understand before. Then sit and listen.

The questions you encounter will lead you to a greater understanding of God.

As we close this chapter, I am reminded of the book of Job. There comes a point in the story when the dialogue has just finished between Job's friends and Job. God has been silent through the entire exchange. Finally, in chapter 38, the Bible says (emphasis mine), "Then the Lord spoke to Job out of the storm. He said: 'Who is this that obscures my plans with words without knowledge? Brace yourself like a man; *I will question you*, and you shall answer me.'"[15]

> THE QUESTIONS YOU ENCOUNTER WILL LEAD YOU TO A GREATER UNDERSTANDING OF GOD.

Over the next four chapters, God asked Job ninety-three questions. Not one time did God give Job the answers that Job was seeking. Rather, in God's questions, he revealed more about himself. In chapter 42, the passage ends with Job replying to the Lord, "Surely I spoke of things I did not understand, things too wonderful for me to know. You said, 'Listen now, and I will speak; I will question you, and you shall answer me.' My ears had heard of you but now my eyes have seen you.'"[16]

Did Job physically see God? No. But through the trials, the questions, and the dialogue, he gained a greater understanding of God. Could it be that the situation you're facing is divinely designed by God so that you can know him in a greater way? Could it be that all of God's questions are personal invitations for dialogue? Could it be that you are on the edge of an incredible breakthrough with God, but you have to answer one question first: "Will you trust me?"

Personal Reflection/Group Discussion

1. What situations are you facing today where God is asking, "Will you trust me?"

---

2. Where do you turn when you get stressed (it could be friends, food, alcohol, the Bible, a family member, and so on)? Identifying where we go when we're stressed can also pinpoint areas where we don't trust God. God wants you to trust him. When you pinpoint these areas, listen closely for God's faith question.

---

3. Describe a recent event where you trusted God. What lessons did you learn, and how will this event shape the way you view more trials in the future?

_____

_____

_____

_____

_____

_____

_____

_____

3 A Grace Question

After years of listening to preaching, we start to pick up the lingo. Pastors speak of love, faith, joy, grace, fellowship, missions, evangelism, discipleship, and so on. Not only do we recognize the words, but we also associate the words with certain types of stories. The following is a typical sermon illustration about grace:

> Charles Spurgeon and Joseph Parker both had churches in London in the 19th century. On one occasion, Parker commented on the poor condition of children admitted to Spurgeon's orphanage. It was reported to Spurgeon however, that Parker had criticized the orphanage itself. Spurgeon blasted Parker the next week from the pulpit. The attack was printed in the newspapers and became the talk of the town. People flocked to Parker's church the next Sunday to hear his rebuttal.
>
> "I understand Dr. Spurgeon is not in his pulpit today, and this is the Sunday they use to take an offering for the orphanage. I suggest we take a love offering here instead." The crowd was delighted. The ushers had to empty the collection plates 3 times. Later that week there was a knock at Parker's study. It was Spurgeon. "You know Parker, you have practiced grace on me. You have given me not what I deserved, you have given me what I needed.[1]

It is a fantastic story about two giants of the faith. However, most grace stories set up the same way. There is conflict between two or more parties, grace is extended by at least one party, and there is recognition of grace (after the fact). In some ways, grace has been pigeonholed into a forgiveness genre.

For many Christians, it's hard to see where forgiveness ends and grace begins. Forgiveness is an act of pardoning. In the story above, grace could be defined as withholding what is deserved to give what is needed. That seems rather forgiving.

When grace is spoken of in reference to salvation, it is often defined as God's unmerited favor. God withholds the punishment we do deserve (death or separation from God), and he gives us what we really need (forgiveness and eternal life).[2] Once again, grace seems to be connected to forgiveness.

While both usages are theologically sound, are we only seeing one aspect of grace and not the fullness of grace if we stop there?

For just a moment, let's walk through several passages on grace:

- **Paul told believers in Corinth, "Concerning this I implored the Lord three times that it might leave me. And He has said to me, 'My grace is sufficient for you, for power is perfected in weakness.'"[3]**

- **The writer of Hebrews encouraged believers, "Therefore let us draw near with confidence to the throne of grace, so that we may receive mercy and find grace to help in time of need."[4]**

- **In his farewell address to the believers in Ephesus, Paul said, "I commend you to God and to the word of His grace, which is able to build you up and to give you the inheritance among all those who are sanctified."[5]**

When suffering from a thorn in the flesh, God promised Paul that his grace was sufficient. When drawing near to the throne of grace, believers are told that they will find grace to help in time of need. When addressing believers in Ephesus, Paul said that the word of God's grace "is able to build you up and to give you the inheritance." Grace is what we need in suffering. Grace is what we need in distress. Grace is what we need to be built up.

Based on these verses, it seems that our understanding of grace can be broadened a bit. Grace is God's unmerited favor, and grace is withholding what we deserve to give us what we need. However, grace is also God's enabling. Watchman Nee said, "Grace means that God does something for me."[6]

In this chapter, we are exploring the boundaries of grace by asking a grace question. To set up this question, we're going to walk through the first part of 2 Timothy. Some preliminary information will provide the context.

Second Timothy is Paul's final letter just before his death. While writing this letter, Paul is in prison facing imminent execution. He knows that his life is coming to an end, and he tells Timothy, "I have fought the good fight, I have finished the course, I have kept the faith."[7]

Before he dies, he has some final words for Timothy. Timothy was special to Paul. He was a constant companion and a faithful minister. When Paul was in prison and unable to check in on a church, he sent Timothy. When Paul needed to correct false teaching in a church, he would send Timothy. When Paul needed to get word out to Christians or to encourage leaders, he knew that he could count on Timothy.

But as good, faithful, and helpful as Timothy had been, he was still very young. He was inexperienced and prone to discouragement. He had been a part of Paul's life, but he had not lived Paul's life. As Paul writes this final letter, it is for the purpose of encouraging Timothy and preparing him for life and ministry without his mentor.

Beginning in 2 Timothy 1:1–2, let's work our way through the first nine verses of the book: "Paul, an apostle of Christ Jesus by the will of God, according to the promise of life in Christ Jesus, To Timothy, my beloved son: Grace, mercy and peace from God the Father and Christ Jesus our Lord."

After introducing himself as the writer and Timothy as the recipient, Paul shares a thought from God (emphasis mine): "Grace, mercy and peace from God the Father and Christ Jesus our Lord."

Paul did not say, "May God's grace, mercy, and peace be with you." As nice as that sounds, it would have been encouragement from Paul. Instead he said, "Grace, mercy and peace from God." The source is different. The source is not Paul; the source is God. In other words, "Timothy, I've been with the Father, and he wants me to tell you, 'Grace, mercy, and peace.' " Grace, mercy, and peace from God the Father and Christ Jesus our Lord. Paul continues in 2 Timothy 1:3, "I thank God, whom I serve with a clear conscience the way my forefathers did, as I constantly remember you in my prayers night and day."

It is one thing to have someone say, "I'm praying for you." Christians say that to each other all the time. It is another thing to have your mentor say, "I am constantly praying for you night and day." Imagine how encouraging that statement must have been to young Timothy.

Paul was not only praying for Timothy; Paul was longing to see Timothy. The text says, "Longing to see you, even as I recall your tears, so that I may be filled with joy."[8] I have some heroes in the faith. I feel honored every time I get a chance to be with them. But I am usually the pursuer. I go to where they are. I call them. I write them. I try to stay in touch, and I'm totally okay with that.

Do you know what's really cool though? Those times when I'm just going about my day and out of the blue they call or write. It's hard to describe how it feels to know that they made the effort to contact me.

In this passage, Timothy's mentor, his friend, his father-in-the-faith says, "Timothy, I'm praying for you night and day, and I can't wait to see you in person." From this point, Paul begins to encourage Timothy:

> For I am mindful of the sincere faith within you, which first dwelt in your grandmother Lois and your mother Eunice, and I am sure that it is in you as well. For this reason I remind you to kindle afresh the gift of God which is in you through the laying on of my hands. For God has not given us a spirit of timidity, but of power and love and discipline.[9]

Paul was praying for Timothy. Paul was longing to see Timothy. Now we see Paul encouraging Timothy.

He reminds Timothy of his faith and the fact that he comes from a family of faith. He then encourages him to stir up that gift because God has not given him a spirit of fear but of power, love, and discipline.

We don't know the exact circumstances that led to these verses. However, we can guess that the circumstances were not good. It is not necessary to stir up the gift of faith unless your faith has been rocked in some way. Paul moves from a challenge to stir up your faith to a challenge to join with him in suffering: "Therefore do not be ashamed of the testimony of our Lord or of me His prisoner, but join with me in suffering for the gospel according to the power of God."[10]

If Timothy wasn't afraid before, he would have reason to fear after this verse. I've recruited a lot of people for positions of service. As a pastor, you recruit people to teach, lead, set up, participate in outreach ministries, follow up with guests, and more. But I have never baited the hook by saying, "Join with me in suffering for the gospel." Paul has been stoned, shipwrecked, whipped, bitten, imprisoned, and deserted.[11] And his invitation is "Why don't you join me?" It's no wonder Paul told Timothy to take a little wine for his stomach's sake.[12] He made that poor boy a nervous wreck.

But did you notice the final part of 2 Timothy 1:8? "Join with me in suffering for the gospel *according to the power of God* [emphasis mine]." Paul is not suggesting that he or Timothy has the ability to do this in his own power. If they are to be used by God in a mighty way, it will be because they are serving "according to the power of God." We're going to come back to this in a moment.

This next verse helps us see why God chose us: "Who has saved us and called us with a holy calling, not according to our works, but according to His own purpose and grace which was granted us in Christ Jesus from all eternity."[13]

This verse marks a major transition. Paul has moved from being the encouraging mentor to the guy next to him in the trenches. Notice the wording [again, emphasis mine]: "Who has saved *us* and called *us* … not according to *our* works." He's not saying, "I'll be praying for you when all hell breaks loose." The wording is "I'm right here with you. I know the suffering. I know the calling. I know the pressure. We are in this together."

This phrase is important for another reason. We know that we are called into relationship with God. However, it's not because of anything we brought to the table. God was not in heaven saying, "What am I going to do? I need a preacher for Las Vegas. Where am I going to find one of those? Maybe Paul Gotthardt would be willing to help me out."

God did not save us or call us according to our works or our ability, or because of our merit; he saved and called us *according to his own purpose and grace.*

There's that word again. Grace!

> GOD DID IN US AND FOR US
> WHAT WE COULD NOT
> DO ON OUR OWN.

As we've already discussed, grace has been defined as God's unmerited favor or withholding what we deserve to give us what we need. I suggested we broaden that definition to include God's enabling. Here's the definition I'm going to use in this chapter: *Grace is God's unmerited favor through which he does in, through, and for us what we cannot do for ourselves.* Let's apply this definition to several key areas of grace:

We could not save ourselves, but God did in us and for us what we could not do on our own. That's grace![14]

We cannot live the Christian life, but God does in us and through us and for us what we cannot do for ourselves. That's grace![15]

We cannot develop the character of Christ on our own. God does in us and for us what we cannot do for ourselves. That's grace![16]

We cannot do the work of ministry in our strength, but God does through us and for us what we cannot do for ourselves. That's grace![17]

The fullness of grace seems to be absent in much of the church. Grace is more than a covering for sin or a manifestation of forgiveness. Grace is the essence of God living through us. It is God doing in, through, and for us what we cannot do for ourselves. Let's make this really personal:

Are you struggling with an addiction? You don't need more determination; you need grace.

Are you in a pit of depression and anxiety? You don't need another pep talk; you need grace.

Are you caught in a sinful, destructive cycle?

Are you battling a prolonged illness that's stealing your joy?

Is your marriage on the rocks?

Are you unable to release jealousy, bitterness, or anger?

Is there a challenge that you don't have the strength to overcome?

Whatever it is, you don't need a pastor giving you a devotional nugget and telling you to think positive thoughts. You need grace. You need the enabling of God to do in you and through you and for you what you cannot do yourself.

Were it not for the grace of God, we would all be in trouble. Notice how Paul fluctuates between highs and lows through the rest of 2 Timothy 1. He speaks of …

the lows of suffering (verse 12);

the highs of God's ability (verse 12);

the lows of remembering sound words in difficulty (verse 13);

the highs of being entrusted with heaven's treasure (verse 14);

the lows of most of his friends deserting him (verse 15); and

the highs of one friend sticking with him (verses 16–18).

Life is going to be a mixture of highs and lows, good and bad, and blessing and suffering. But when Paul writes 2 Timothy 2:1, he tells Timothy how to go through it all, "You therefore, my son, be strong in the grace that is in Christ Jesus."

"Timothy, if you're going to run the race set before you, if you're going to rise above your fears, if you're going to keep your sanity, if you're going to maintain your passion for God and your joy, don't miss this truth. Be strong in the grace that is in Christ Jesus."

That brings us to our grace question. It doesn't matter if you're enjoying a period of victory or begging for God's help in the valley, God is continually asking his people,

> **"ARE YOU DEPENDING ON YOURSELF OR ON ME?"**

This question brings us back to grace.

To experience the enabling grace of God means that we rely upon him even when we think we're strong. It means we move away from self-reliance, and we cultivate a life of God-dependence. It means we pray before, during, and after a trial. It means we chase after, rely on, and trust in him at all times.

In the spring of 2005, I was in my garden. For those who live outside of Las Vegas, you would probably call the adjoining piece of land behind your house a yard. For those who live in Las Vegas, it's difficult to call a fifteen-by-thirty-foot patch of grass and rocks a yard. So I'm in my garden, and it had been a tough week. A number of new problems had appeared, I had become discouraged, and I had decided to call it a day. I went to the garden to do a little work and to process the events with God.

As I was "processing the events with God" (code for complaining), this thought came to mind. "You worry about things you own." Based on my level of anxiety, I owned everything!

I was worried about the finances of the church, people in the church, a meeting location for the church, developing small groups in the church, the ongoing growth of the church, mission partnerships for the church, and the list could keep going. The statement grabbed my attention. "You worry about things you own."

I would say things such as, "God, this is your church," but I worried as if it were mine. In the garden, I can remember telling God, "If it's your church, you have to build it. If it's not your church, I have no right trying to hold it up." At that moment, God gave a sense of peace that's hard to describe.

The moment of elation lasted a few minutes, and then reality hit again. There's still a message to prepare. There's still the need for another meeting location. We still have leaders to develop and ministries to start and resources to locate. I could feel the anxiety growing, and then this question came to mind, "Are you depending on yourself or on me?"

As long as I depended on myself to do everything and provide everything, the anxiety was heavy and palpable. When I focused on God as the giver of grace, peace would return.

A second way that God drove this point home was through counseling. Before coming to Las Vegas, most of my counseling was focused on marriage counseling, financial counseling, and helping people with depression, anxiety, or questions about the Christian life. When I came to Las Vegas, not only did the amount of counseling increase but also the type of counseling changed. It seemed like everyone who came for help was struggling with some form of sexual addiction.

I approached this counseling the same way I did all of the rest. I learned some basic information about their lives, their spiritual condition, their struggles, and the things they had tried to do to overcome the addiction. I directed them back to prayer and to time in Scripture. I encouraged them to find an accountability partner. We talked about avoiding the things that fueled the addiction and adding things that would reprogram their mind. In other words, I loaded them up on a list of good things to do and not do.

People did everything I told them to do, but they came back more discouraged than ever. Their addiction was like acid; it had the ability to eat through their spiritual routines.

I didn't know what else to do. In seminary, I took a course on pastoral counseling. It covered the bare basics. Although I will admit that I was absent once or twice, I don't remember anyone addressing this subject.

I prayed about what to do. I looked through my counseling books and jotted down ideas. I was preparing to launch my second attack. As I prayed, I said, "God, what have I missed? These people are doing the right things, but it's not helping. What do I tell them?" Instead of giving me an answer for them, this thought came to mind: Are you depending on yourself or me?

He had me again. I was depending on *my* books, *my* counseling experience, *my* seminary training, *my* techniques, *my* wisdom, and *my* systems. I was at the center of the counseling. My prayer was, "God, deliver them." My approach was, "Paul, it's up to you."

I was frustrated because I didn't feel that I was trained to operate in grace. I didn't know how to rest in the enabling of God and to rely on his strength. I was trained to have the answer. I was trained to use the right tools and follow the right procedures. I was trained to find good resources and offer them to those in need. I didn't know how to operate in grace. If I could develop the counseling classes in seminary, there would be two levels:

- Pastoral Counseling 101: People Need God
- Pastoral Counseling 201: You Are Not God

As honestly as I can say it, I didn't know how to depend on God in this way. If I took my plans out of counseling, it was going to be a really short session. The person would tell me about their problems, I'd get a really spiritual look on my face and say, "Only God can help you. Have a wonderful day!" Not exactly a recipe for effective counseling! But in some ways, it would be true. My efforts failed, their efforts failed, accountability failed, counseling techniques failed, religious rituals failed. Nothing worked!

People kept coming to me for help, and I couldn't find any programs in town that had a solid record of success. Finally, I decided to make grace-based counseling the focus of my PhD work. I spent four years reading, researching, praying, and developing a grace-based recovery plan that brings healing to those struggling with sexual addiction.

Here's the cool thing. As I incorporated principles of grace into my counseling, the results were staggering. People who had struggled for ten or twenty years were breaking free. People who hadn't had a single week of victory in five years were passing the six-month mark and the one-year mark. One by one the chains began to fall off. God was restoring broken lives. Marriages were coming back together. People were experiencing victory for the first time, and none of it was about me, my counseling, or their efforts. God was doing in and through and for them what they could not do themselves. People were learning to depend on God instead of themselves. People were walking in grace!

The lessons God taught me about grace spread to everything else. Grace became the central theme in all of my counseling. It gave solid direction to some of the other difficult issues of life. How do you help someone forgive a spouse when trust has been shattered? How do you help someone experience peace when they are prone to anxiety? What do you do when someone is about to make a life-altering decision, and they've been warned repeatedly about the consequences? In each area, we have to depend on God and that dependence positions us in the flow of grace.

Grace became a central theme in my personal walk with God. I moved away from trying to discipline myself into holiness, and I began to rest in God's enabling.

Grace has become a major component of the DNA of our church. When plans fall through, resources are needed, volunteers are short, or spiritual attacks pop up, the question comes back, are you depending on yourself or me? So often the answer is "God, I'm sorry. I'm depending on myself again."

Let me be quick to say that it's not easy to shift from self-reliance to God-dependence. Most of the time, I feel like God has to corner me in a difficult situation to show me the frailty of my efforts. Grace is not comfortable. But grace is necessary.

For the rest of your life, God will ask the simple question: "Are you depending on yourself or on me?" In what areas are you still trying to do it yourself?

Are you frustrated by self-effort? Are you ready to step into a greater level of freedom? Then be encouraged by a man who "fought the good fight … finished the course [and] kept the faith."[18]

"You therefore, my son, be strong in the grace that is in Christ Jesus."

When you find that you're depending on yourself instead of God, let your next thought be, "God, I can't, but you can through me." Solomon warned about relying on ourselves instead of God. Proverbs tells us, "Trust in the Lord with all your heart and do not lean on your own understanding. In all your ways acknowledge Him, and He will make your paths straight."[19] By recognizing our limitations, humbling ourselves before God, and trusting in his ability instead of our own, we have positioned ourselves in the channel of God's grace. James wrote that "God is opposed to the proud, but gives grace to the humble."[20]

As long as we feel that we can do it ourselves, we get locked in a circle of pride. We alienate ourselves from the grace we need. Apart from God's enabling, this cycle is predictable and permanent. The following two figures are modified versions of Clyde Cranford's circles of pride and humility. Take a look at how this cycle unfolds, starting with "Temptation" at the top and working clockwise around the circle.

This circle represents the recurring issue of pride. Regardless of the tempta- tion (the temptation to do for God, to impress God, or to avoid sin), pride is built on self-reliance. The only way to break free from the pride circle is to walk in humility and to be infused by the grace of God.

If pride is the glue that holds the previous circle together, then humility must be key to breaking the cycle. The goal of the counselor is to help the person struggling with deep sin to recognize the destructive cycle, pride's hold, and humility's need. However, the greater need is to help this person realize his or her need for Christ. Humble people can still be enslaved to sin if Christ is not living inside of them. Christ is the answer, but humility is the path to his victory. It looks like this:

This circle represents the victorious path of grace. The believer who learns to rely upon God and not themselves is infused with God's grace. God does in, through, and for them what they could not do for themselves. They get the victory. God gets the glory!

What trial are you facing? What challenge is keeping you awake at night? What set of circumstances are you powerless to change? Listen to the gen- tle voice of God: "Are you depending on yourself or on me?"

Personal Reflection/Group Discussion

1. Based on the definition of grace shared in this chapter, list some of the victories and advancements God has brought into your life.

_____

_____

_____

_____

_____

_____

_____

2. What current challenge(s) are you facing that require God to do in you, through you, and for you what you cannot do for yourself?

_____

_____

_____

_____

_____

_____

_____

3. In your life, how has God emphasized the importance of you relying on him and not on yourself? List any events, thoughts, or lingering questions that suggest he's teaching you grace.

_____

_____

_____

_____

_____

_____

_____

_____

A Contentment Question

In the July 27, 1992, edition of *U.S. News & World Report*, Amy Bernstein wrote an article entitled, "Dream On." The article focused on generational expectations and what's required to achieve the American dream.

According to Bernstein, postwar Americans had always cherished the expectation that their standard of living would improve with each generation. At the beginning of the Reagan era, two of every three respondents in a poll said they expected to be better off than their parents. Yet by 1992, a shift had occurred and that figure was reversed. Almost 75 percent of the 1,000 people who answered the poll said the American dream was "harder to attain" than it was a generation ago.

The pollsters took the question one step further by asking people to define in monetary terms what it would take to achieve the American dream. The answers were interesting. For Americans with household incomes under $25,000, the average number was $54,000 a year. For those who made $100,000 or more, the average number was $192,000. In other words, regardless of where a person is economically, our personal version of the American dream seems to be about twice as much as we're currently making.

I can identify with this article. When my family lived in North Carolina, our house had three bedrooms, 1,300 square feet, and no garage. My prayer at the time was, God, if we could have one more bedroom, 2,000 square feet, and a one-car garage, I'd be content. Today, our house has four bedrooms, over 2,400 square feet, and a two-car garage. Guess what my prayer is now? "God, if we could have one more bedroom, a three-car garage, and half an acre of land, I'd be content."

Discontentment seems to manifest itself in that little voice that says our lives would be perfect if we had just a little more, a little newer, a little faster, a better upgrade, a bigger something. Sadly, when we're constantly striving for the next thing, we rarely enjoy what we currently possess. Benjamin Franklin once said, "Content makes poor men rich; discontent makes rich men poor."

In this chapter, we're dealing with a contentment question. Many people are surprised to learn that God says a lot about contentment in the Bible. People are equally surprised to learn that God is not against people having possessions, reaching goals, and enjoying the finer things of life. However, he does have a problem when our pursuit shifts from him to something else.

Most of the time, the shift is subtle. I don't think people consciously say, "God, I'm putting you to the side while I pursue something else." We just get distracted, sidetracked, and off course. It is so easy to move away from our pursuit of God. I believe these are some common ways we tend to lose focus:

- **Instead of pursuing God, we pursue the promotion at work.**

- **Instead of spending time with God, we give our free time to personal ambitions and hobbies.**

- **Instead of planning ahead of time to meet with God in the early morning, we stay up late watching TV and are too tired to get up the next day.**

- **Instead of desiring a deeper relationship with him, we get sidetracked by things that are temporal.**

We spend our energy, time, and resources pursuing newer things, bigger things, or better things. All the while, we're hoping that these things will bring satisfaction.

Again, I want to be careful to point out that God is not against people having things. In fact, Scripture clearly indicates that God has a track record of blessing his people with possessions. In the following passages, notice the generosity of God toward his people:

- "The Lord has greatly blessed [Abraham], so that he has become rich; and He has given him flocks and herds, and silver and gold, and servants and maids, and camels and donkeys."[1]

- "Then it shall come about when the Lord your God brings you into the land which He swore to your fathers, Abraham, Isaac and Jacob, to give you, great and splendid cities which you did not build, and houses full of all good things which you did not fill, and hewn cisterns which you did not dig, vineyards and olive trees which you did not plant, and you eat and are satisfied, then watch yourself, that you do not forget the Lord."[2]

- "David was prospering in all his ways for the Lord was with him."[3]

- "God said to Solomon, '… I will give you riches and wealth and honor, such as none of the kings who were before you has possessed nor those who will come after you."[4]

The gifts of God can bring enjoyment, pleasure, opportunities, and responsibility. However, material wealth and possessions were never intended to become our pursuit or joy. Scripture clearly speaks to this subject as well:

- "And he said to them, 'Take care, and be on your guard against all covetousness, for one's life does not consist in the abundance of his possessions.' "[5]

- "But those who desire to be rich fall into temptation, into a snare, into many senseless and harmful desires that plunge people into ruin and destruction."[6]

- "No one can serve two masters, for either he will hate the one and love the other, or he will be devoted to the one and despise the other. You cannot serve God and money."[7]

While God may choose to bless some with possessions, he does not intend for the possessions to bring ultimate satisfaction. That form of satisfaction can only be found in relationship with him. Religion will never satisfy this need. Spirituality will never satisfy this need. People will never satisfy this need. Things will never satisfy this need. God alone can fill that need. Take note of where fullness of joy and satisfaction are found (emphasis mine):

- "You make known to me the path of life; *in your presence* there is fullness of joy; *at your right hand* are pleasures forevermore."[8]

- "As for me, *I shall behold your face* in righteousness; when I awake, I shall be satisfied *with your likeness.*"[9]

- "Keep your life free from love of money, and *be content with what you have,* for he has said, '*I will never leave you nor forsake you.'* "[10]

THINGS CAN MAKE A SATISFIED LIFE MORE ENJOYABLE, BUT THINGS CAN NEVER MAKE A DISCONTENTED LIFE SATISFIED.

In this chapter, we are going to read the story of a man who learned how to enjoy life while finding unshakable contentment in Christ. That's key! God's not presenting an either-or scenario. He's not saying, "In order to be content, you must give away everything you have, never have fun, never set goals, and never strive for something more." What is clear through Scripture is that God alone can fully satisfy.

Things can make a satisfied life more enjoyable, but things can never make a discontented life satisfied.

Our story is centered on the apostle Paul. In many ways, Paul's story reads like a novel. There are adventures and hardships, twists and turns, accomplishments and life lessons. Here's the quick version.

Paul was born in Tarsus of Cilicia into a proud and strict Pharisee family. He was a Roman citizen by birth; he was highly educated under the great rabbi

Gamaliel; he spoke several languages fluently; and he held himself to an extremely rigorous standard of Jewish law.

We know through some of his writings that he had misgivings about his ability to keep every part of the law, but he always understood that the law was good and had a purpose.[11]

When we first encounter Paul in the Scriptures, he was intent on destroying the revolution started by Jesus. By his own admission, he persecuted followers of Christ.[12] When the first Christian martyr was killed, Paul was an approving onlooker. He was so determined to root out and destroy this spurious sect that he sought approval to round up followers of Christ, imprison them, beat them, and bully them (even to the point of death).[13]

On one of these missions to eradicate Christians, Paul encountered the risen Christ on the road to Damascus. The entire story is found in Acts 9. Starting in verse three, the Bible tells us that "a light from heaven flashed around him; and he fell to the ground and heard a voice saying to him, 'Saul, Saul, why are you persecuting Me?'"[14] Paul didn't recognize the voice, but Jesus identified himself and told Paul to get up, enter the city, and wait for further instructions. Paul was blinded during the encounter and after was led by the hand into the city. While Paul was praying, he was given a vision of a man named Ananias who would come, lay hands on him, and restore his sight. While he was having the vision of Ananias, God was speaking to Ananias about Paul. Ananias went to the house and laid hands on him, and God restored his sight. Paul's conversion changed the course of Christianity and civilization itself.

After this encounter, Paul spent almost three years in the Arabian Desert, followed by some time in Jerusalem visiting Peter and James. After spending time with Peter and James, Paul spent a number of years in Cilicia where he preached the gospel and supported himself by making tents.[15]

His missionary journeys began almost fourteen years later when he was called by Barnabas to help the congregation in Antioch carry out its mission.[16] They ministered and helped in Antioch for a while, and eventually they were sent by the church in Antioch on a preaching mission through

Cyprus and Asia Minor. Everywhere Paul preached, either revival or riots broke out. His message of Christ-crucified split synagogues. His message of salvation by grace enraged some Christians who were still convinced that a person was required to keep the law in addition to having faith in Christ. Paul became a polarizing figure wherever he went.

As a result of his incredible conversion and controversial message, there was always excitement surrounding his journeys. On one occasion, he was stoned and left for dead. On another occasion, he was beaten within an inch of his life. He was run out of towns, shipwrecked, imprisoned, and forgotten by close friends. When he started churches, he encountered internal opposition. When he preached in synagogues, he encountered outward opposition. Everywhere Paul went, he saw either incredible miracles or debilitating problems.

But through it all, God used Paul. Paul wrote almost half of the books in the New Testament, started strategic churches in Europe and Asia, and personally influenced many of the initial church leaders. Years later, he was beheaded by Nero with only a handful of friends around him. Now you have the overview of Paul's life.

I think it's important for people to know Paul's story before reading Paul's writings. It's easy for us to dismiss some of Paul's writings by saying, "That's easy for Paul to say because he's never gone through what I'm going through. He's never faced the trials I'm facing. He's never endured the people I'm around. He could be content because everything in his life was just peachy." History tells a different story.

Now that you know the context of Paul's life, I want to walk you through several passages in the book of Philippians. Philippians is a letter that Paul wrote to the church in Philippi while he was in prison in Rome.

He started the church in Philippi almost ten years prior to writing this letter. The Philippian believers had generously supported Paul when he left Philippi. They were always concerned about his well-being, but for almost two years they had lost touch with Paul altogether.

They finally heard that after his arrest in Jerusalem, he had been transferred to a prison in Rome. In an amazing act of love and humility, they sent a messenger (Epaphroditus) to Paul with a word of encouragement and a financial gift. They apologized for losing contact with him and for being unable to support him financially for those two years.

The book of Philippians is Paul's response to that church. He thanks them for their gift, identifies Christ as the only true source of joy, and then shares what God taught him about contentment while experiencing the ups and downs of life.

There are several key texts to which I want to draw your attention. Let's begin in Philippians 1:1–4:

> Paul and Timothy, bond-servants of Christ Jesus, To all the saints in Christ Jesus who are in Philippi, including the overseers and deacons: Grace to you and peace from God our Father and the Lord Jesus Christ. I thank my God in all my remembrance of you, always offering prayer with joy in my every prayer for you all.

We can see that from the beginning, Paul's tone is thankfulness and joy. In fact, the concepts of joy or rejoicing are found sixteen times over the next four chapters.

PEOPLE FALSELY ASSUME THAT THEY WOULD BE CONTENT IF THEIR CIRCUMSTANCES WERE DIFFERENT.

Let's move forward to Philippians 1:12: "Now I want you to know, brethren, that my circumstances have turned out for the greater progress of the gospel." The key word is "circumstances". We need to talk about this word because circumstances are often connected to contentment. People falsely assume that they would be content if their circumstances were different. Paul had an amazing understanding of circumstances.

Paul understood that there are two main ways through which God accomplishes his will on earth: miracles and providence.

Miracles are God's direct, sovereign intervention into the natural world. It is an event so contrary to the normal course of events that there is no scientific or naturalistic explanation other than the power of God. Notable miracles include the parting of the Red Sea, the plagues of Egypt, the actions of the prophets, biblical healings, and raising the dead.

Providence is not miraculous in the sense that it does not interrupt the natural order. It allows for all the circumstances, events, people, decisions, and elements of normal life. However, God supernaturally weaves them together to fit his exact purpose. Solomon spoke of God's providence.[17] The stories of Esther and Joseph speak of God's providence.

Understanding God's providential control is critical to contentment. Paul was content in his current circumstances because he understood "my circumstances have turned out for the greater progress of the gospel." He understood that God was doing things behind the scenes that he could not fully see or know but he could trust.

In Philippians 1:21, Paul writes, "For to me, to live is Christ and to die is gain." To live is Christ. Let that concept sink in! To live is Christ. Paul is saying that his pursuit, his joy, his being, his passion, his life is Christ. His life is not ministry. His life is not hobbies or things. His life is Christ. Therefore, if he lives, he enjoys Christ. If he dies, he enjoys Christ. There's no way he can lose.

Moving along in the letter to the Philippians, we find an interesting statement in Philippians 3:1: "Finally, my brethren, rejoice in the Lord. To write the same things again is no trouble to me, and it is a safeguard for you." The Amplified Bible translates the same verse, "Delight yourselves in the Lord and continue to rejoice that you are in Him." Paul is saying, "Let your joy be found in Christ." Continue reading in Philippians 3:4–6:

> Although I myself might have confidence even in the flesh. If anyone else has a mind to put confidence in the flesh, I far more: circumcised the eighth day, of the nation of Israel, of the tribe of Benjamin, a Hebrew of Hebrews; as to the Law, a Pharisee; as to zeal, a persecutor of the church; as to the righteousness which is in the Law, found blameless.

Paul just gave us a short list of his credentials. He followed the right commands. He was born into the right family. He did what the law required.

He was zealous, committed, and blameless. That sounds great. But did it satisfy? Verses 7–11 will give Paul's assessment:

> But whatever things were gain to me, those things I have counted as loss for the sake of Christ. More than that, I count all things to be loss in view of the surpassing value of knowing Christ Jesus my Lord, for whom I have suffered the loss of all things, and count them but rubbish so that I may gain Christ, and may be found in Him, not having a righteousness of my own derived from the Law, but that which is through faith in Christ, the righteousness which comes from God on the basis of faith, that I may know Him and the power of His resurrection and the fellowship of His sufferings, being conformed to His death; in order that I may attain to the resurrection from the dead.

In one paragraph, Paul rejects all of his past, accomplishments, and self-righteousness and says, "It's nothing compared to Christ. Everything I gained, I now view as loss. Those things never filled me. They never satisfied. They are garbage compared to what I've found. I'd gladly lose everything so that I might gain him."

It is from that perspective and with that background that we come to the words of Philippians 4:11–13:

> Not that I speak from want, for I have learned to be content in whatever circumstances I am. I know how to get along with humble means, and I also know how to live in prosperity; in any and every circumstance I have learned the secret of being filled and going hungry, both of having abundance and suffering need. I can do all things through Him who strengthens me.

This text is one of the greatest passages on contentment in our Bibles. It's fantastic because it clarifies so many of the misunderstandings about contentment. Paul helps us see that contentment is not something you wake up with; you learn it. In verse 11, he says, "I have learned to be content." Through all of the ups and downs, beatings and imprisonments, miracles and providence, Paul learned contentment. There is no such thing as a wasted experience.

He also helps us to see that circumstances have nothing to do with contentment. In verse 11, he emphatically declares, "I have learned to be content in whatever circumstances I am." Contentment is not what you experience when everything lines up the way we want it to. It's not even about circumstances. You can be content in whatever circumstances you're in.

It is also good to see that contentment is not about God taking everything from you. For those who think contentment is found in having nothing, Paul would reject that idea. He said in verse 12, "I know how to get along with humble means, and I also know how to live in prosperity; in any and every circumstance I have learned the secret of being filled and going hungry, both of having abundance and suffering need." God taught Paul contentment on both ends of the spectrum. Contentment is not about how much you have but who has you.

That brings us to a final thought. Contentment is found in Christ. "I can do all things through Him who strengthens me." Philippians 4:13 could be one of the most misquoted verses in Scripture. We use this verse as a superman text or as a pick-yourself-up pep talk. Paul is not saying, "I can do anything! Bask in my awesomeness! I'm Paul the super apostle and missionary-extraordinaire. I can do it! I can do it! I can do it!" This text isn't even about Paul.

The focus is on Christ. He is saying, "I can face every challenge, I can climb any mountain, I can live under any circumstances, I can enjoy every moment, I can do all things—*through him who strengthens me*." The secret is "through him." As long as he has Christ, he can face anything.

Only God can fully satisfy. Things can make a satisfied life more enjoyable, but things can never make a discontented life satisfied.

All of this leads to our contentment question. God has asked this question at so many critical places in my life:

"WHEN WILL JESUS BE ENOUGH?"

"Paul, when will your joy and satisfaction come from me? When will you stop looking for fulfillment in degrees, knowledge, accomplishments, people, positions, numbers, success, growth, and everything else? When will Jesus be enough?"

God ingrained this truth in me in one big way. I refer to it as the "85 principle."

Life Baptist Church officially launched as a church on October 3, 2004. From that Sunday through the end of the year, we averaged 85.46 people on Sunday morning. Please don't make fun of the .46 people. When you're a church planter, you take every percentage you can get. There were thirteen Sundays from the launch through the end of the year.

In 2005, we averaged 85.78 people on Sunday morning. For fifty-two Sundays, twelve months, one full year, we averaged 85.78 people per Sunday.

For the first fourteen weeks of 2006, I need to simply give you the numbers for full effect. Our attendance was eighty-five, ninety-five, eighty-eight, eighty-five, eighty-three, ninety-three, eighty-seven, eighty-five, ninety-two, ninety, ninety-three, one hundred, and eighty-two.

For the first fourteen weeks of 2006, we averaged 88.78 people. You might think, "Well, it's moved up! That's good!" When you're a church planter, and you're genetically wired for numbers and growth, do you know what 88.78 translates into? Eighty-five people.

For basically seventy-nine weeks, one and a half years, we could not budge the number, fudge the number, force the number, manipulate the number, or forget the number. Believe me, I tried.

We would have a thirty-person mission team show up to help us for a week. They would worship with us on Sunday. I'd get so excited and think, "This week, we're going to have at least 115 people." Sunday would come, and thirty of our regular people would get sick or be on vacation. The count would be eighty-five people.

I would have weeks where a family would call and say, "We're going to be out of town this weekend. Can you find replacements for where we serve on Sunday?" I'd get another call, then another call, and another call. I would start adding up the people and count as many as forty of our regulars who were going to be gone. I'd start to panic and think, "We're not even going to hit eighty-five this weekend. There's going to be like, forty of us at church." I would dread that Sunday. Sunday would come, and forty visitors would show up. Once again, we were at eighty-five people.

We distributed mailers to 40,000 homes. According to the marketing specialists, we could expect anywhere from a half percent to 1 percent of recipients to walk through the doors on Sunday. One half percent of 40,000 is 200. But Sunday came, and we had eighty-five people. Of the eighty-five, five were guests, and three hadn't even received a mailer.

We would not be discouraged. Our original staff of four would fill up our camel packs with water, prayer walk neighborhoods, and distribute thousands of flyers personally. The following Sunday we would have eighty-five people.

It was almost like God was playing a game with us. "Hey Paul, how many other ways would you like to get to eighty-five?"

I was so focused on breaking the "eighty-five barrier" that my focus shifted from *God* to *growth*. I couldn't enjoy being with God because every conversation I had with him was, why aren't we growing? I couldn't enjoy being with Brea and the girls because even though I was in the room, my mind was focused on getting past the eighty-five barrier. I couldn't enjoy what God was doing in *some* areas because I was distracted by what he hadn't done in *this* area.

I was obsessed with attendance, numbers, and growth. As I wrestled with God, I kept hearing the same question: "When will Jesus be enough? Stop worrying about attendance. That's not your problem. When will your joy come from me, not how many show up on Sunday? When will you be satisfied in me, not in your idea of success?"

Every time God asked the question, he was helping me identify things in my life that had interrupted my pursuit of him. Have you noticed a trend in most of the questions?

Will you pursue *me* in the process of whatever you're going through? Will you trust *me*? When will *Jesus* be enough? They all lead back to God.

God's questions are establishing a testimony for us. It's a testimony that can endure any problem, excel in any situation, overcome any obstacle, and find contentment regardless of the circumstances. What is the testimony?

> HE IS NOT A GREAT
> ADDITION TO OUR LIFE.
> HE IS OUR LIFE.

"To live is Christ." He is our life. He is not a great addition to our life. He is our life.

When Paul addressed believers in Colossae, he said, "When Christ, who is our life, is revealed, then you also will be revealed with Him in glory."[18]

- **"To live is *Christ*."**

- **"When *Christ*, who is our life."**

- **"I can do all things through *Him* who strengthens me."[19]**

When will Jesus be enough? What has distracted you from pursuing Christ? What is getting in the way of you pursuing him completely? Where are you searching for satisfaction? Only God can fully satisfy. Things can make a satisfied life more enjoyable, but things can never make a discontented life satisfied.

The psalmist spoke with much wisdom when he said, "Whom have I in heaven but you? I desire you more than anything on earth."[20]

Personal Reflection/Group Discussion

1. You can assess your relationship with God better than anyone else. Are you content with Christ? If not, what are you pursuing instead of him?

_____

_____

_____

_____

_____

_____

_____

_____

2. Based on Paul's story, what does it look like to be content in Christ?

_____

_____

_____

_____

_____

_____

_____

3. When will Jesus be enough? This question can only be answered when you are honest with yourself. Don't force the answer because you want to be correct; prayerfully answer the question because it holds the keys to contentment.

_____

_____

_____

_____

_____

_____

_____

_____

4. Describe the difference between godly contentment and spiritual apathy.

_____

_____

_____

_____

_____

_____

_____

_____

5 A Control Question

Imagine for a moment that you're in a counseling session. You're sitting on a couch; there's a therapist in the chair next to you; and the therapist says, "Do you think you have some control issues?" How would you respond? There are some people who are painfully aware of their control issues. They would immediately say yes because they see the way their desire for control has adversely affected their lives. However, the rest of us are either unaware of our control issues, or we have deceived ourselves into thinking that we have none.

A number of years ago, Jeff Foxworthy created a comedy empire around the phrase, "You might be a redneck if … " He would finish the phrase with hundreds of funny and sometimes very insightful thoughts. For instance, "You might be a redneck if you've been married three times and still have the same in-laws," or "You might be a redneck if you think possum is 'The Other White Meat.' "

I could keep myself entertained for hours with those things. Which might be the real joke itself! "You might be a redneck if you can keep yourself entertained for hours with these jokes." Anyway, take that format, and let's see if some people are simply unaware of their control issues. "You might have control issues if … "

- **"You might have control issues if you're never able to completely release a project to others."**

- **"You might have control issues if you constantly feel the need to force your agenda."**

- **"You might have control issues if you pray about an issue and then immediately try to solve the problem yourself."**

- **"You might have control issues if your prayer life consists of telling God what to do, how to do it, when to do it, and why it needs to be done."**

- **"You might have control issues if your life is consistently characterized by stress, anxiety, and sleeplessness."**

- **"You might have control issues if you vehemently fight the notion of having control issues."**

You get the point. There are a few people who are genetically laid-back. God has blessed them with a temperament that stays calm regardless of the situation. There are others who are artificially laid-back. They have chosen to alter their state of mind through prescription or illegal drugs. Then there is the rest of us. We think we're relaxed, and we want to be relaxed, but inwardly we crave control. That's not all bad.

Some control is necessary for basic living. Eating right, exercising, and getting enough rest controls some health issues. Using budgets, living within our means, and keeping our kids from swinging on the chandeliers are necessary forms of control. Without some control in our lives and in our homes, we would live in a regular state of chaos.

Likewise, local government maintains basic societal control. I'm glad that we have law enforcement, government officials, checks and balances, and a judicial system to help keep control within our communities. Without societal control, people would do what was right in their own eyes. The book of Judges shows the results of that mind-set.

We clearly need control to function in society. The question is, how do we respond to those things that are outside of our control?

There's a quote that has become extremely popular over the years. You see this quote on cards, plaques, pictures, and refrigerator magnets: "God, grant me the serenity to accept the things I cannot change, courage to change the things I can, and wisdom to know the difference." There is a lot of wisdom in those words.

The quote has been called "The Serenity Prayer." It was written by Reinhold Niebuhr in 1926 and was adopted by Alcoholics Anonymous and other twelve-step programs. What most people do not realize is that the three statements mentioned above are not the full quote. Here's the full quote:

> God, grant me the serenity
>
> to accept the things
>
> I cannot change,
>
> Courage to change the
>
> things I can, and the
>
> wisdom to know the difference.
>
> Living ONE DAY AT A TIME;
>
> Enjoying one moment at a time;
>
> Accepting hardship as the
>
> pathway to peace.
>
> Taking, as He did, this
>
> sinful world as it is,
>
> not as I would have it.
>
> Trusting that He will make
>
> all things right if I
>
> surrender to His Will;
>
> That I may be reasonably happy
>
> in this life, and supremely
>
> happy with Him forever in
>
> the next. Amen.[1]

When the entire quote is read, it shifts from a general quote about God to a very specific quote about Christ. "Taking, as He did, this / sinful world as it is ... Trusting that He will make / all things right if I / surrender to His Will." As you read the entire quote, you get a better idea of what it means to "[accept] the things I cannot change." Niebuhr speaks of accepting hardships, taking this sinful world as it is, and surrendering to God's will. Regardless of whether you are reading the shortened version or the full version, they both speak to an issue we all face daily. Where is the line between healthy and unhealthy control?

When our lives drift to the unhealthy side of control, the symptoms are often insecurity, worry, fear, anger, manipulation, confusion, and being overwhelmed. There are repercussions to unhealthy control. When our lives align with the healthy side of control, we enjoy the benefits of discipline, structure, peace, responsibility, and accomplishment. There are benefits to healthy control.

So where's the line? How do we take responsibility for our lives without feeling the need to micromanage and manipulate everything around us? How can we learn to live securely with things we cannot control? The Bible gives us some of those answers.

In this chapter, we are going to focus on a familiar text in Matthew 11:28–30. As we go through the text, prepare yourself to answer a control question. The passage says, "Come to Me, all who are weary and heavy-laden, and I will give you rest. Take My yoke upon you and learn from Me, for I am gentle and humble in heart, and you will find rest for your souls. For My yoke is easy and My burden is light."

Matthew 11 is a chapter of challenge. Jesus challenged John the Baptist in verses 1–6 for taking offense with him. Jesus challenged the crowds in verses 7–19 for not listening to John the Baptist. Jesus rebuked some cities in verses 20–24 for failing to repent after witnessing numerous miracles. The tone of the chapter is very serious.

But then we come to Jesus' prayer to the Father, and his appeal to those who are burdened and weary. It's in this appeal that we can gain some much-needed perspective about control. For the Christian, control can only be understood through our relationship with Christ.

In this passage, Jesus addresses people who are weary, worn-out, and burdened by trying to do things their way. Some of their weariness comes from life and the difficulties it brings. Based on the context, however, it seems that Jesus is specifically referring to those who are worn-out from trying to be right with God through their actions. They believed that doing the right things would please God and, subsequently, bring them peace.

Instead of bringing peace, it only brought a greater burden. Their actions were never good enough. They still messed up. The stress of trying and failing only led to further frustration and greater weariness.

Jesus sees this group wearied by efforts, and he says, "Come to Me, all who are weary and heavy-laden, and I will give you rest."

The word *weary* does not describe a moment of discomfort; it describes a state of perpetual fatigue and working to utter exhaustion. *Heavy-laden* speaks of a great load being placed upon an already wearied person. The word *rest* is not just release from work; it carries the idea of rejuvenation. Jesus is saying, "Not only will I bring you out of this perpetual weariness, and not only will I remove the heavy load from you, but I will also rejuvenate your life." He releases the burden; he restores our strength.

The invitation is "Come to me." The offer is genuine rest. But the condition is found in verse 29.

In verse 29, Jesus says, "Take My yoke upon you and learn from Me, for I am gentle and humble in heart, and you will find rest for your souls." The Jews used the phrase *the yoke* to describe the act of entering into submission to something. When you submit to something, what do you give up? Control! The Jews spoke of submitting to the yoke of the law, submitting to the yoke of the kingdom, submitting to the yoke of God, and submitting to the yoke of the rabbi.

In Jesus' invitation to come, it is with the understanding that those who do come are entering into submission to his yoke. A rabbi's yoke was his specific teachings and understanding of God's law.

Jesus says, "Take my yoke upon you [submit to my teachings] for My yoke is easy." The word *easy* is not being used as the opposite of hard. It means "well-fitting." In the region of Palestine during the first century, oxen were connected with a yoke made of wood. When fitting an ox for a new yoke, the owner would bring the ox to the carpenter. The carpenter would take exact measurements of the animal, and then he would build a yoke specific to that ox.

The imagery is extremely powerful. Jesus is saying, "I can see you're weary. I can see you're burdened. The reason you're tired is because the yoke you're currently wearing was never made for you. The yoke of the law was given as a teacher to lead you to me. Take my yoke upon you. It is custom-made for your life."

Let's bring all the pieces together. The invitation is "Come to me." The offer is genuine rest. But the condition is submitting to Christ's yoke. To enter this relationship and to enjoy Christ's rest, we are giving up control. We are submitting to him.

> ONCE WE ENTER THE YOKE OF CHRIST, WE ARE NEVER REMOVED FROM THE POSITION OF SUBMISSION

When Jesus says, "Come to Me, all who are weary and heavy-laden, and I will give you rest," the next line is not, "After you come, try to figure the rest out yourself, get right back in the game, make the right decisions, do the right things, and solve the problems as best you can." *Once we enter the yoke of Christ, we are never removed from the position of submission.*

All Christians experience peace *with* God because of Christ, but many lack the peace *of* God because they're consistently trying to re-establish control of their lives.

Maybe they thought that God's offer was forgiveness without further contact. Maybe they thought God would stay confined to the "spiritual" part of their lives, but they would still control the rest. Maybe they thought Christ was just going to empower and bless their plans. Whatever the initial premise might have been, when Christians are struggling to control their lives, they are misunderstanding the nature of the relationship between God and themselves.

When we submit to God, we submit all of who we are and receive all of who he is. We become a new creation.[2] It's a divine takeover. Therefore, it's no longer my money, my time, my house, my job, and my family. It's all God's!

Paul told believers in Corinth, "You are not your own[.] For you have been bought with a price."[3] When Paul addressed the church in Galatia, he said, "It is no longer I who live, but Christ lives in me."[4]

The Christian life is not me living for God; it's God living through me, and that's not a bad thing.

In fact, the only reason Christians can have peace of mind is because we have a relationship with the one who controls everything:

- **God controls the world.**[5]

- **God controls the human heart.**[6]

- **God controls the times and seasons.**[7]

- **God controls the weather.**[8]

- **God controls the appointment of kings and deposing of leaders.**[9]

Notice the way King David described God's complete control in 1 Chronicles 29:11–12 (The Living Bible):

> Everything in the heavens and earth is yours, O Lord, and this is your kingdom. We adore you as being in control of everything. Riches and honor come from you alone, and you are the Ruler of all mankind; your hand controls power and might and it is at your discretion that men are made great and given strength.

As Christians, we understand that God has ultimate control of our lives and everything that happens around us. When we enter relationship with Christ, we submit to his yoke and give up our quest for control. For the rest of our lives, we are never removed from the position of submission. He is sovereign; he is Lord; he is God.

It is by virtue of this relationship that we can enjoy peace that surpasses all understanding.[10] There is something freeing about knowing that the final outcome of our specific problems is not resting on our shoulders, but this understanding does not mean that we are to sit idly and do nothing. While God is in complete control, he gives believers responsibility as outlined in the Bible.

Colossians 3:2 says, "Set your mind on the things above, not on the things that are on earth." As followers of Christ, we have the responsibility to set our minds on the things above.

Colossians 4:2 says, "Devote yourselves to prayer." As followers of Christ, we have the responsibility to devote ourselves to prayer.

Colossians 4:6 says, "Let your speech always be with grace." As followers of Christ, we have the responsibility to respond to others in grace.

As God lives in you and through you, he directs us to our responsibilities while reminding us of his complete control. You and I may not be able to control what happens to us, but we can set our minds on things above. We might not be able to control the circumstances, but we can devote ourselves to prayer. We might not be able to control what others say to us or about us, but we can speak to others with grace.

The line between healthy and unhealthy control is found between two principles: God controls everything, and as a believer, I have responsibilities outlined in the Bible.

That brings me to the control question. When you're in that moment of trying to discern what to do, and you're trying to get things done, and circumstances and people are out of control, how do you gain perspective? Here's a question that God seems to ask with that end in mind:

"WHAT HAVE I ASKED YOU TO DO?"

Remember, the exact wording of these questions will change from person to person, but the essence of the question will be the same. As you abide in relationship with God, his Spirit will prompt you through prayer and through the Bible. These promptings may be strong or gentle, but we need to listen.

I cannot tell you how many times I've heard God's Spirit whisper these thoughts into my heart. "I know things haven't worked out the way you hoped. But what have I asked you to do? I know how hurtful that situation is, but what have I asked you to do? I know that you're confused, you're upset, and you want to control the situation, but what have I asked you to do?"

So often during these times of prayer, God directs me back to Scripture I just read, a passage I memorized, or a biblical principle he recently taught. As I obey his word, I experience peace.

The first time I really remember God bringing me face-to-face with this question was August 27, 2004. On that morning, I was trying to pray, but I couldn't keep a cohesive thought. I had so many things running through my mind that my attention was constantly shifting from one thing to another.

Whenever my mind is overwhelmed like that, the only thing I can do is write my thoughts down on paper. I pulled out a journal and began to write every thought, every need, and every to-do item connected with work, personal improvement, and my family. I wrote down everything that people told me I had to be or do in order to be a good pastor, a good Christian, and a good husband and father.

For almost an hour, I wrote down fifteen personal concerns, twenty-six family concerns, and eighty-nine work-related concerns. There were 130 identifiable issues that were pressing for my time and attention.

Contained within this list were things I was told I needed to be or do. For example, if I was going to be a good pastor, I needed to be a soul-winner, a visionary, a discipler of people, a reader, more accessible, a lifelong student, a counselor, a theologian, a peacemaker, more gracious, more loving, more passionate, more giving, a shepherd to the community, and in contact with church-planting partners. I needed to plant more churches, do more follow-up, prepare insightful messages, be a man of prayer, guard my family time, send in state reports to the Nevada Baptist Convention, build relationships, and the list just kept on going. That is just twenty-two items out of the eighty-nine things on the work list. There were still fifteen other personal concerns and twenty-six other family concerns.

When I finished the list, it was the first time that the weight of expectations really hit me. When I tried to focus on getting better in one part, it seem liked something else would suffer. When I tried to be more focused on prayer, it seemed like relationships would suffer. When I tried to be intentional about sharing the gospel, I missed developing leaders. When I attempted to spend time with family, I felt guilty for saying no to church things.

I don't know if it's the same way in other professions, but as a pastor, I felt that if I could not sustain the workload, I was letting God down. He called me into ministry. He knows the demands of ministry. If I couldn't meet the demands, I failed.

For the first time, I had a moment of unbelievable clarity. "I cannot do it! There is no way I can fulfill every expectation. There's not enough time in the day to do everything that needs to be done. As soon as one project is completed, twenty others take its place. I cannot control or accomplish the 130 things spinning in my head at this moment."

And no sooner did that thought come into my mind than the words of Matthew 11:28–30 followed: "Come to Me, all who are weary and heavy-laden, and I will give you rest. Take My yoke upon you and learn from Me, for I am gentle and humble in heart, and you will find rest for your souls. For My yoke is easy and My burden is light."

At first, there was a sense of peace. Could Jesus really be inviting me into a life of rest? But that sense of peace was quickly followed by confusion. I can remember thinking, "Either Jesus is lying, or I have greatly missed the Christian life. I'm a Christian, but I'm not experiencing rest. I have followed Christ, but this path isn't easy. The burden is not light. How can this statement be true?" And then the question came!

"Paul, what have *I* asked you to do?" This path isn't about what the books say, or friends say, or seminary professors say, or you say. "What have *I* asked you to do?" The first thing Jesus said is "Come to me." I didn't have 130 things to do. I had one thing to do. I needed to be with Christ. I soon learned that while I'm with him, he directs me to do what he wants me to do.

When I understood this thought, other passages began to jump off the pages of Scripture. While Jesus is calling the twelve disciples in Mark 3, verse 14 tells us, "He appointed twelve, so that they would be with Him and that he could send them out to preach." What was their job? To be with him! What was Jesus' job? To send them out when the time was right.

John 15 gives the vine and branches analogy. Jesus said in verse 5, "I am the vine, you are the branches; he who abides in Me and I in him, he bears much fruit, for apart from Me, you can do nothing." What is our part? We are to abide in Christ. What is Christ's part? He will bear fruit through us.

The more I understood the connection, the more I gained valuable perspective on control. God's question was simple. "What have I asked you to do?" Regardless of the situation, regardless of the pressure or the circumstances, go back to this question. "What have I asked you to do?" If we do not answer his question first, we will inevitably return to our quest for control.

When God asks that question in my life, my answer is always the same: "To be with you!" Intimacy with God is the primary call for every believer. As I am with him, he will give me whatever assignments he desires. As I obey the promptings of God, I have the security of knowing that I'm doing what he desires, and everything is still under his control.

The further I walk with God, the more convinced I am of the following truth: Everything God desires to do in and through my life, he will accomplish out of the overflow of my relationship with him. Everything!

Do you find yourself losing sleep and becoming anxious and trying desperately to gain control? Remember the key concepts from this chapter:

1. As a Christian, we are never removed from the position of submission.

2. God controls everything.

3. We relinquish control when we enter relationship with Christ.

4. As we abide in Christ, he will direct us to our responsibilities as outlined in the Bible.

5. As we obey, we experience the peace of God.

Let God's simple question resonate in your heart: "What have I asked you to do?"

Personal Reflection/Group Discussion

1. Based on the teachings of this chapter, what set of circumstances are you facing today that seem overwhelming?

_____

_____

_____

_____

_____

_____

_____

_____

2. What areas of your life are you trying to control but without much success?

_____

_____

_____

_____

_____

_____

3. Make a list of the things demanding your time, attention, and resources.

_____

_____

_____

_____

_____

_____

4. Can you effectively accomplish and personally control everything you listed under number three? If so, how? If not, what can you do?

_____

_____

_____

_____

_____

_____

6 A Patience Question

There's an ongoing joke among pastors (and a lot of church members, for that matter) that regardless of the text, the subject, or even the one delivering the message, every sermon has three points and a poem. You could preach John 3:16 or the entire book of Revelation, and you will get the same format. While I've delivered my fair share of three-point messages, I'm not huge on poetry. I fear that I have left our church poetically deficient. However, for the sake of adding a little culture to this book, I'd like to share a small poem. It's a poem about patience. It has no title or known author, but it makes a lot of sense. It goes like this:

Patience is a virtue,

Possess it if you can.

Found seldom in a woman,

Never in a man.

And there you go! I hope your life has been enriched and filled with warm fuzzies.

Patience is a virtue! If I had a nickel for every time my parents quoted that phrase, I'd at least have a couple of bucks to go with the grief of that statement. When you're forced to exercise patience, all you want is a little understanding, not a tagline to remind you that you're waiting. Let me share two examples.

You're a kid, and it's three weeks before Christmas. For at least the past two months, every store has pushed a Christmas theme. Every commercial on TV is about Christmas sales. Every book you're reading in school is about Christmas. It seems like the whole world is saying, "Focus on Christmas." But the days are dragging by. You know that life would be a little more bearable if you could just open one present. You ask your parents if you can open one gift, and they say, "It's good to wait for things. Besides, patience is a virtue." Can I tell you something that would be more virtuous? Opening a present!

Or you're on a twelve-hour road trip. You and your siblings are packed into the back of a station wagon. You've got an elbow in your side, a book bag on your feet, and a Big Gulp in your stomach. You say, "It's crowded back here. Are we there yet?" And your dad says, "When I was a kid, it was never crowded in the car because we walked everywhere. Be thankful you're not walking. And remember, patience is a virtue."

Patience is a virtue.

Could no one think of anything else good to say about patience? You'd think that with all the waiting, someone would think up another one-liner. Well, I've got a statement for you. It's not quite as catchy, but it's at least accurate.

Learning patience stinks! But it can be beneficial.

We've been addressing the teaching techniques of God, and specifically the way he questions his people. So far, we've dealt with a relational question, a faith question, a grace question, a contentment question, and a control question. Now, I want us to spend some time with a patience question.

Before we jump into a text, I want to give you my goal for this chapter. You need to know where we're going before we reach our destination. Let me start with what we're *not* doing. I'm not trying to persuade you to "hang in there just a little longer." You've heard those pep talks. They give you a solid ten minutes of hope before reality hits. I'm also not sharing the story of a Bible hero who was so patient that he amplifies our impatience. Therefore, we will not discuss Job. Finally, I'm not giving three points that no one is going to remember after they finish this chapter. Here's my goal: I want to make the waiting just a little bit easier.

You're still going to need to wait. You're still going to hear people say, "Patience is a virtue." You're still going to feel out of control. But as a Christian, we need to look at things from a slightly different perspective. We understand that everything that touches our lives is filtered through the loving hands of God. He is in absolute control. When God requires us to exercise patience, we are not waiting for the stars to align, circumstances to change, or people to do what they need to do. We are waiting for God to say *now*.

I've learned a valuable lesson from personal experience. Waiting on God is a little easier when you see the benefits that come to those who are patient.

The primary text for this chapter is Psalm 40:1–3. The writer is King David. Altogether, there were at least forty different people that God used to write the sixty-six books of our Bible. Without question, David wrote more on the subject of waiting on God than any other biblical writer. He speaks of it at least twenty-six times in the Psalms alone:

- **He waits on the Lord and encourages others to do the same.**[1]

- **His soul waits for the Lord.**[2]

- **He encourages us to rest in the Lord and wait patiently for him.**[3]

- **His soul waits in silence for God.**[4]

Yet when you read about David's life in 1 and 2 Samuel, 1 Kings, and 1 Chronicles, you are immediately aware that waiting for anything is not a part of David's nature.

When David was sent by his dad to check on his brothers in battle, he heard Goliath taunting the armies of God saying, "I defy the ranks of Israel this day; give me a man that we may fight together."[5] Instead of waiting for more information or to see what others would do, the Bible says, "Then David left his baggage in the care of the baggage keeper, and ran to the battle line."[6] He ran to be a part of the action.

You may remember the rest of the story. David accepted the challenge of Goliath. When he showed up to fight, Goliath taunted David in front of everyone. Then David gave one of those memorable speeches that essentially says, "You're a punk; your time is up; and you're going down." The next phrase in 1 Samuel 17:48 says, "David ran quickly toward the battle line to meet the Philistine."

I like a guy who not only takes on a giant but who also just can't wait to get started. David was a doer, and not just in this situation:

- **When a bear attacked his sheep, David killed it.**[7]

- **When Goliath challenged Israel, David accepted.**[8]

- **When Israel went to battle, David led them.**[9]

- **When Bathsheba was bathing, David took her.**[10]

- **When Bathsheba got pregnant, David eliminated her husband.**[11]

- **When someone wronged him, David prayed that calamity would befall them. He prayed that God would kill, silence, break, and despoil them, and then wipe their names from the history books.**[12]

- **When the temple was to be built, David had the plans drawn up, the money raised, the uniforms designed, and every detail in place.**[13]

David was not a sit-on-the-sideline-pet-your-puppy-and-hope-things-are-going-to-work-out type of guy. He was a runner. He was a doer. He was a leader. He was a problem solver. Did I mention he was king? How many kings are known for waiting on anything?

Yet David wrote more about waiting on God than any other biblical writer. God constantly placed him in situations that required him to wait, and I'm convinced God taught him a lot on the subject along the way. We don't know if God taught David to wait while he was a shepherd, a fugitive, a king, or a little of all three. But we know one thing for sure. David was convinced of the benefits of waiting on the Lord.

Let's read several verses on the subject and discover some of the benefits for ourselves. Beginning in Psalm 40:1–3, David writes,

> I waited patiently for the Lord; and He inclined to me and heard my cry. He brought me up out of the pit of destruction, out of the miry clay, and He set my feet upon a rock making my footsteps firm. He put a new song in my mouth, a song of praise to our God; many will see and fear and will trust in the Lord.

It's been said that David wrote this psalm after running from his son Absalom, who was trying to kill him. There's not a lot of evidence to either confirm or deny this claim, but it is apparent from the context that David had just faced a huge challenge, and he was now waiting on God.

I like this text because David describes what God did in his life as he waited. The Hebrew translation for "I waited patiently" is literally "waiting, I waited." Waiting on what? Waiting on God, I waited. The reason that distinction is so important is because it emphasizes why David waited and possibly what God was teaching. This wasn't an exercise in waiting so that he could just learn to be patient. He waited because he was convinced that only God could solve his problem.

> DAVID WAITED BECAUSE HE WAS CONVINCED THAT ONLY GOD COULD SOLVE HIS PROBLEM.

That concept puts a completely different spin on patience. Does God teach patience for patience's sake? Or does God teach patience so that we will learn to have complete confidence in him?

Now David looks back over this time of waiting, and he shares five wonderful benefits he received by waiting on the Lord.

First, he received the benefit of being heard by God (Psalm 40:1). Don't let the simplicity of this statement undermine its powerful truth. It actually addresses one of our greatest needs while waiting. When you are waiting on God and praying and searching for answers and hoping things will change and begging God to do something and do it quickly, there is a tendency to interpret God's silence as a lack of interest. "God, will you please help? I've got nowhere else to turn. [Long period of silence.] God, are you even listening to me? [Silence and frustration.] God, are my prayers making it past the ceiling? Do you hear me? [Silence and despair.]"

Let David's phrase wash all over you for a moment. He writes in verse 1, "I waited patiently for the Lord; and He inclined to me and heard my cry." The word *inclined* means "to lean into." He's saying, "When I waited on the Lord, he didn't ignore my prayers. Instead, the creator of the universe, the king of heaven, leaned into me, and heard my faintest cry."

Be encouraged when you're waiting on the Lord. God hears your every prayer. What was a second benefit of waiting on the Lord?

Being delivered by God (Psalm 40:2). As David looked back over that period in his life, he says it was like being stuck in a pit or a swamp. No matter how hard he tried, he couldn't get out. But instead of continuing to kick and struggle, David waited patiently on the Lord, and he put his trust in God's strength.

> GRACE IS ABOUT TRUSTING, NOT TRYING.

The more Christians grow in their understanding of God's grace, the more we see that grace is about trusting, not trying. It's about resting in him, not wrestling with the problems and issues we encounter every day.

David waited on the Lord, and verse 2 gives a benefit of that waiting. "He brought me up." What brought him up? Was it self-will? Was it determination? Was it a friend, more money, a new job? No. "He brought me up out of the pit of destruction, out of the miry clay." God delivered David. What happened next?

Continuing in verse 2, we see the third benefit: God established David. "And He set my feet upon a rock making my footsteps firm." There are some truths that are best understood only through experience. This is one of those statements.

When people feel as though their lives are spiraling out of control, we instinctively try to change course. But new turns often come with new challenges. They may come in the form of work problems, health problems, relational problems, financial problems, spiritual problems, or take other forms. As a new wave of problems arrive, people scramble for a safe place. They search for something stable in their lives—something that will not move while they regain their bearings.

David writes that when he waited patiently on the Lord, "[God] set my feet upon a rock making my footsteps firm."

> WHEN YOU'VE BEEN SLIPPING INTO A PIT, YOU WILL PRAISE GOD FOR A FIRM PLACE TO STAND.

At one point, he's sliding further into a miry pit. The next moment, God pulls him out and sets his feet on a firm foundation. God established David. When you've been slipping into a pit, you will praise God for a firm place to stand.

The fourth benefit of waiting on the Lord was that God gave David a testimony (verse 3). After this experience, David's life would never be the same. He waited patiently on the Lord, and the Lord "put a new song in my mouth, a song of praise to our God." This concept is so great to me.

There are a lot of things I hear and see as a pastor. As a pastor, you're with people in their greatest moments and during their deepest trials. You see people on their best days, and you see them on their worst days. Do you know what I've never heard? I've never heard someone say, "I waited on God, and I have more problems to show for it." But I have heard a lot of people say just the opposite. "I didn't wait on God, and now I've got more problems than I can handle." When people wait on the Lord, he puts praise on their lips.

What other benefit of waiting on the Lord did David discover? He learned that God uses the testimony of waiting to lead others to himself. "Many will see and fear and will trust in the Lord" (Psalm 40:3).

This next thought is enough to make you shout for joy and weep with conviction all at the same time. How many people will be led to Christ if you just wait on God? I don't know what you're going through. But what if God uses your patience and your story to lead others to himself?

How many times have you been ready to throw in the towel, but then you heard about the patience of someone else and you kept going? How many times have you been ready to give up on God, but when you saw the faith of someone else, you gained strength to pursue?

A couple of weeks ago, a lady asked me if I've read the book *Tortured for Christ*. She was almost speechless after reading what Christians have endured for the sake of Christ. She encouraged me to read it. I started the book. The author describes life in Romania in the early 1950s while the country was under Communist control. Here are two small excerpts:

> One of our workers in the Underground Church was a young girl. The Communist police discovered that she secretly spread Gospels and taught children about Christ. They decided to arrest her. But to make the arrest as agonizing and painful as they could, they decided to delay her arrest a few weeks, until the day she was to be married. On her wedding day, the girl was dressed as a bride—the most wonderful, joyous day in a girl's life! Suddenly, the door burst open and the secret police rushed in.

> When the bride saw the secret police, she held out her arms toward them to be handcuffed. They roughly put the manacles on her wrists. She looked toward her beloved, then kissed the chains and said, "I thank my heavenly Bridegroom for this jewel he has presented to me on my marriage day. I thank Him that I am worthy to suffer for Him." She was dragged off, with weeping Christians and a weeping bridegroom left behind…her bridegroom faithfully waited for her. After five years she was released—a destroyed, broken woman, looking thirty years older. She said it was the least she could do for her Christ.[14]

How many prayers do you think her fiancé prayed? How many prayers for release and protection do you think her family and friends prayed? How many agonizing nights did they wonder if God was listening, if God could see what was happening, and why he wasn't doing something? They were forced to exercise patience. Here's the second excerpt:

> It was strictly forbidden to preach to other prisoners, as it is in captive nations today. It was understood that whoever was caught doing this received a severe beating. A number of us decided to pay the price for the privilege of preaching, so we accepted their terms. It was a deal: we preached and they beat us. We were happy preaching; they were happy beating us—so everyone was happy.
>
> The following scene happened more times than I can remember. A brother was preaching to the other prisoners when the guards suddenly burst in, surprising him halfway through a phrase. They hauled him down the corridor to their "beating room." After what seemed an endless beating, they brought him back and threw him—bloody and bruised—on the prison floor. Slowly, he picked up his battered body, painfully straightened his clothing and said, "Now, brethren, where did I leave off when I was interrupted?" He continued his gospel message!

These are just two stories of people who waited on God for years, in agonizing conditions, with little or no encouragement from friends and family. But their testimonies in the end are not angry, bitter, or resentful. Their testimony is "Praise to our God. Many will see it and fear and will trust in the Lord." But you don't have to be tortured by Communists for God to build a testimony of patience through you.

- **You may be waiting on God to heal your marriage.**

- **You may be waiting on God to provide for a need.**

- **You may be waiting on God for a child, a spouse, or direction for your future.**

- **You may be waiting on God for a job, good health, or strength to make it one more day.**

Regardless of what you're waiting on, God can use your testimony of waiting to bring others to himself. But it all depends on whether we make the choice to wait on the Lord.

So I have a patience question for you. It's a question that God continually asks his people amidst the challenges of everyday life.

"WILL YOU WAIT ON ME?"

God knows the process seems slow. God knows that you get nervous. He knows that you want to do something. But if you will just wait on him, he's got something greater.

How many waiting testimonies is God building today? How many people are about to be pulled out of a miry pit, if they choose to wait just a little longer? How many people are just days away from a solid rock? There's nothing I can share to make the wait shorter, but there's a lot we can learn to make the wait better.

In Psalm 40:1–3, David helps us recognize five benefits of waiting on the Lord. But that is not an exhaustive list. There are other benefits found in different parts of Scripture:

- **Waiting leads to expectancy: Ps. 5:3; Rom. 8:23; 1 Cor. 4:5; Gal. 5:5; and Titus 2:13.**

- **Waiting leads to hope: Ps. 33:20 and 130:5; Isa. 51:5; and Mic. 7:7.**

- **Waiting leads to trust: Isa. 8:17.**

- **Waiting leads to patience: Rom. 8:23–25.**

While all of these are great, they may pale in comparison to what David learned. He learned to have complete confidence in God.

God has been teaching this exact lesson to our church for more than seven years now. When we first arrived in Las Vegas, we began praying that God would give our church a place of permanency. Trying to start a church in

Sin City is hard enough; trying to purchase real estate in the fastest growing city in America for over seventeen years was next to impossible. We found that commercial real estate in southwest Las Vegas was selling for $1.4 to $1.8 million per acre. In order to build a basic, multipurpose building for church, we would need at least two to three acres of land.

We knew that apart from the intervention of God, a place of permanency would never become reality. Our only option was to pray and pray hard.

We prayed as a core group. We asked our prayer partners to pray for the same thing. Over thirty mission teams came to Las Vegas to help us in the first three years. We asked each of these teams to pray that God would provide a place of permanency.

Not only did we ask people to pray, we asked them to pray specifically. We asked God to burden the heart of a landowner or builder who needed a tax write-off to give us five acres of land in the southwest part of the city. We needed the land to be west of I-15, north of Blue Diamond, east of Durango, and south of Spring Mountain. We were very specific in our prayers.

For a couple of years, we prayed and nothing seemed to happen. Actually, something did happen. The price of land went up. That wasn't exactly the trend we were looking for. We waited patiently and prayed like crazy.

After two and a half years, God chose to answer our prayers. I received a call on a Friday afternoon. For the sake of anonymity, we will refer to this person as Bob. Bob said, "You probably don't know me. I don't attend your church, and I don't believe we've met. But God has burdened my heart. I'm supposed to buy your church a piece of land. Would you be willing to come to my office so we can discuss some details?"

I'm pretty sure I blacked out for about thirty seconds, but once I regained my composure, I agreed to come—immediately!

When I arrived at Bob's office, he shared a little more of the backstory. Bob was a builder in Las Vegas, and he had been tremendously blessed by God through the housing boom. He needed a tax write-off for that year and felt burdened to purchase five acres of land for our church. Due to his knowledge of the market and his connections with landowners who bought most of the property twenty years ago, he felt confident that he could secure the land we needed for around $400,000 per acre. At this point, he laid a map out in front of me and said, "Point to the area you want, and we will take it from there."

God had answered our prayers. Everything lined up. It was a builder who came forward. Bob needed a tax write-off. He wanted to give our church five acres of land, and we were even able to pick our location. Everything was perfect. We waited patiently, and God heard our cry.

But the lesson on patience was not over. For the rest of that year, we tried to purchase land, but nothing worked out. At the end of the year, Bob put $2 million in a trust fund for the church because he needed the tax write-off for that year. The money was in the bank. Now we just needed to find the land.

Over the course of the next three years, we looked for property, we prayed over property, we put in offers on property, but we didn't get a piece of property. Who knew that the biggest obstacle to securing land in Las Vegas was getting someone to take our money?

We didn't see what God was doing at the time, but we can definitely see it today. God was not only teaching us patience and trust and developing us spiritually as a church, but he was also protecting us from a huge mistake. Had we purchased property from 2005 to 2010, we would have paid too much for the land, and it would have lost significant value in the real estate collapse.

However, when the time was right according to God's plan, he allowed us to purchase 4.4 acres of land in 2011 for $767,000. The land is exactly where we needed it, and the lower price allowed us to use the remaining funds to pay for over half of the phase-one construction costs. But the blessing doesn't end there.

For the past four and a half years, we've rented two suites in a professional building for office space, worship space, and classroom space for kids. The combined square footage for both suites is only 3,300 square feet. We run three services on Sunday morning to accommodate a growing church and the lack of physical space. We have kids' classes meeting in hallways, under stairwells, and sometimes outside. The rent for our current facility is $9,200 a month. When phase one of Life Community Center is completed in 2012, we will own a 14,000-square-foot facility (with worship space, church offices, adult classroom space, a kitchen, children's classrooms, a playground, and parking), and our mortgage payment will only be $6,500 a month.

In hindsight, I praise God that everything fell through for several years. I praise God that he cared enough to not give us what we wanted in the moment. I praise God that he is so creative, so powerful, and so gracious that he gives us more than we ask for—just because he can.

> I PRAISE GOD THAT HE CARED ENOUGH TO NOT GIVE US WHAT WE WANTED IN THE MOMENT.

Is God telling you to wait? Are you being forced to exercise patience in a certain area? Does it seem as though God's not listening to your prayers? Do not give up! God's delays are not necessarily God's denials. He is not teaching you patience for the sake of patience; he is teaching you patience so that you might learn to completely depend on him.

As I write this chapter, it has been over eight years since God first began this lesson of patience in the context of a place of permanency. We had to be patient for God to supply the resources. We had to be patient for God to direct us to the land. We had to be patient with the drawings, the permits, selecting contractors, and everything else. The lesson has been steady and constant. "Will you wait on me?"

So how do you live this truth in difficult situations?
I've got a few final thoughts.

First, choose to wait on God. You have a choice to make. You can either wait on God, or you can trust that your wisdom is sufficient to get you through. Just a quick glance at poor decisions in your past should send you running into the arms of God. Take your concerns to God. Make the decision to wait.

Second, reflect on the benefits of waiting. Jot down the benefits of waiting, and put them in places where you will be reminded of them. Write these concepts in your Bible. File them under *P* for "patience" or *A* for "amazingly hard lessons in life" or *I* for "I don't have a clue." I don't care how you file the information away. Do it in a way that's right for you and where you can find it later. Waiting on God is just a little bit easier when you see the benefits of waiting. Remind yourself of the things we've discovered in this passage.

God hears you, he delivers you, he establishes you, he gives you a testimony of praise, and he brings others to himself through your experience. Through it all, he teaches us to have complete confidence in him.

Finally, do not confuse waiting with laziness. G. Campbell Morgan describes what it looks like to wait on God:

> Waiting for God is not laziness. Waiting for God is not going to sleep. Waiting for God is not the abandonment of effort. Waiting for God means, first, activity under command; second, readiness for any new command that may come; third, the ability to do nothing until the command is given.[15]

Waiting on God simply means we are following his lead. Instead of blazing the trail, will you choose to wait on him? Vance Havner said, "He who waits on God loses no time."

Learning patience stinks! But it can be beneficial.

When you're going through those times of waiting, and you're tempted to just do something because fear or anxiety or the pressure is getting to you, listen carefully to God's question. "Will you wait on me?"

Who knows? There may be a $2 million blessing on the other side.

Personal Reflection/Group Discussion

1. Can you hear or sense God telling you to wait on him? List the areas where his voice is clearly being heard.

_____

_____

_____

_____

_____

_____

_____

_____

2. Think over the decisions you regret from the past. Did you choose to act instead of wait? What were some of the short- and long-term repercussions?

_____

_____

_____

_____

_____

_____

_____

_____

3. What lessons has God personally taught you while waiting on him? How many of those lessons correlate with the benefits discovered in this chapter?

_____

_____

_____

_____

_____

_____

_____

4. Who do you know who could benefit from the lessons of this chapter? How can you share this information with them?

_____

_____

_____

_____

_____

_____

_____

7 A Character Question

In the last chapter, we talked about patience and the benefits of waiting on God. When I introduced the subject, I shared a totally awesome poem, and the first line of the poem was, "Patience is a virtue." We discussed how this has become the definitive statement on patience. Patience is a virtue.

In this chapter, we're focused on a character question. The word *character* also has a definitive statement. This statement does not explain character, describe its value, or even make a compelling argument for the necessity of solid character. It's more of a catchall phrase that people use when they don't have anything better to say. Can you guess what it is?

"It builds character!" Have you ever noticed how versatile that phrase can be?

A six-year-old does a swan dive off the top bunk and breaks his arm. The mom freaks out. What does the dad say? "It builds character."

The PE coach tells everyone to run two laps around the football field. It's one hundred degrees outside, and everyone starts to groan and complain. The coach says, "Make that three laps. It builds character."

The parents of a sixteen-year-old girl say, "It's time you get a job." The teenager is taken aback because the current arrangement is pretty sweet: she does her thing and someone else pays for it. The parents go on to say, "You need to take on more responsibility and get a dose of what the real world is like. Having a job will be good for you. Besides, it builds character."

The phrase works for everything. Skinned knees, doing chores, joining the military, stubbing your toe, a financial crisis, the flu—it really doesn't matter. Whatever you're going through, someone is going to say, "Suck it up. It builds character."

With all of the character-building opportunities that we've enjoyed since infancy, we should be character ninjas. George Washington, Gandhi, and Billy Graham all wrapped into one!

But there are at least two problems with the saying: (1.) Saying something builds character and actually building character are two different things. (2.) Who defines character? Are we striving for our parents' definition of character, society's definition of character, or our personal version of what we think character looks like? What is the standard?

For the Christian, our standard is Christ. Romans 8:29 says, "For those whom He foreknew, He also predestined to become conformed to the image of His Son." Another word for image is *likeness*. When a person looks in a mirror, they see the image or likeness of themselves.

According to Scripture, God's plan is that his people are conformed to the image or the likeness of Christ. When people look at you or me, God wants them to see him.

Does this mean we are to take on Jesus' outward appearance? Are we all supposed to grow beards, wear purple robes, and look like artists' renderings of Christ? It would make for a great conversation starter, but I don't think that's the intention. The text is referring to his character. God wants us to be conformed to the character of Christ.

I know that statement sounds "churchy," but it's really important. God's plan is not that you conform to the character of Billy Graham. His plan is not that you become like your parents, mentor, or personal hero. God's plan is not even that *you* become a better version of *you*. God's predestined plan is that we are conformed to the character of Christ.

If we accept this idea, it changes everything about the character discussion.

First, it's no longer about building character in general; it's about building his character within us. The target is defined. Second, it becomes irrelevant to compare our character to another person's. "I know I have issues, but look at that guy. At least I'm not as bad as him." That may be the case, but he is not the goal. God's plan is to conform you to the image of Christ. Third, it's no longer about comparing the *current* me with the *former* me. Sometimes, we can be dazzled by our definition of progress. "Well, I used to be a jerk 100 percent of the time. Now it's only 70 percent." Yes, but God's plan is not that you become a better you; it is that you become like him.

So how do we do that? If you want to be an artist, there are classes that can teach you art. If you want to be a lawyer or a pharmacist, there are universities that train you for those careers. If you want to be organized, there are books, videos, personal coaches, and entire companies created to help you achieve that goal. Where do you go to become like Christ?

The most popular answer people give is to church. We become like Christ by going to church. When I hear that answer, I want to say, "Have you ever been to church?" Some of the most judgmental, backbiting, un-Christ-like people I've ever met are in church. That is by no means a characterization of all churches or all Christians, but being in church does not necessarily produce Christ-like character. Where do you go to become like Christ?

Let's allow Scripture to provide an answer, beginning in John 14:16–17 with the words of Jesus:

> I will ask the Father, and He will give you another Helper, that He may be with you forever, that is the Spirit of truth, whom the world cannot receive, because it does not see Him or know Him, but you know Him because He abides with you and will be in you.

Who is the helper that abides with us and is in us? If you said, "The Holy Spirit," you are correct. The apostle Paul adds to our understanding of the Spirit being in us when he addresses the believers in Corinth. "Or do you not know that your body is a temple of the Holy Spirit who is in you?"[1] The Holy Spirit abides in every believer.

Then in Philippians, Paul says, "For I am confident of this very thing, that He who began a good work in you will perfect it until the day of Christ Jesus."[2] Paul is referring to the character of Christ being formed within us. Who began this good work in you? The answer is the Holy Spirit. Who will complete the work that was begun in you? The answer is the Holy Spirit. Are you seeing a trend here?

Paul goes on to say, "Work out your salvation with fear and trembling; for it is God who is at work in you, both to will and to work for His good pleasure."[3] Note that the verse says, "Work out your salvation," not "Work for your salvation." Salvation is the free gift of God.[4] But we are to work out what God has worked in.

Who is at work in you? The answer is the Holy Spirit, the agent of change within you. He allows us both "to will" (that is, to desire) and "to work" (that is, to be enabled so that we can work) for his good pleasure.

Our final passage is found in 2 Corinthians: "And all of us have had that veil removed so that we can be mirrors that brightly reflect the glory of the Lord. And as the Spirit of the Lord works within us, we become more and more like him and reflect his glory even more."[5] According to this verse, as the Spirit of the Lord works within us, we become more like him. That is transformation.

My next thought is a side note, but it's worth mentioning. I hear people say, "God, we give you glory, or God, I want my life to bring you glory." We use this terminology synonymously with praise, worship, thanksgiving, or gratitude. If we're talking about recognizing God's glorious nature, there is no problem. Scripture tells us to glorify the Lord.[6] However, if we're talking about adding to God's glory, that's a different story.

Glory is an attribute of God.[7] Just as God is completely sovereign, altogether holy, and 100 percent righteous, he is also completely glorious. If humanity failed to recognize his glory, it would not leave him glory-deficient. To say "We give you glory" implies that we can add to his glory. To say "I want my life to give you glory" implies that imperfection can somehow bring glory to Perfection. As we read closely, we see that people can *recognize, relish,* and *reflect* the glory of God. However, we cannot generate glory in and of ourselves. Just as the moon cannot generate light (it reflects the light of the sun), so we cannot generate glory, but we can "be mirrors that brightly reflect the glory of the Lord." How does this happen? As God is at work within us (transforming our character to the character of Christ), we reflect the glory of God.

How do we know that the Holy Spirit is at work within us? Is there a tangible way that we can see God's activity? Yes. Galatians 5 tells us, "But the fruit of the Spirit [or the manifestation of the Spirit's work within us] is love, joy, peace, patience, kindness, goodness, faithfulness, gentleness, self control."[8] The word *fruit* in verse 22 is the singular tense. This verse is not sharing nine disconnected traits; rather, these nine attributes are the singular manifestation of the Holy Spirit within us. When he is working in a person's life, all nine characteristics will be present and growing to some degree.

Compare this list to the character of Christ. Jesus expressed perfect love, unending joy, enduring patience, unparalleled kindness, unquestioned goodness, complete faithfulness, supreme gentleness, and uncompromising self-control. We see these traits lived perfectly in Christ. As the Holy Spirit conforms us to the image of Christ, they will be more pronounced in us.

Based on the six portions of Scripture we've just reviewed, we can say the following: the Holy Spirit starts the work within us, the Holy Spirit continues the work within us, and the Holy Spirit will complete the work within us. How do we know that the Holy Spirit is at work within us? There's spiritual fruit!

If every bit of God's character-transforming work within us points back to the activity of God, what does God require of us? John 15:1–5 provides the answer:

> I am the true vine, and My Father is the vinedresser. Every branch in Me that does not bear fruit, He takes away; and every branch that bears fruit, He prunes it so that it may bear more fruit. You are already clean because of the word which I have spoken to you. Abide in Me, and I in you. As the branch cannot bear fruit of itself unless it abides in the vine, so neither can you unless you abide in Me. I am the vine, you are the branches; he who abides in Me and I in him, he bears much fruit, for apart from Me you can do nothing.

If you continue reading the next five verses, you'll see similar language. Jesus is describing the context of character transformation. He just told us both where to go and what to do in order to become like him. We are to abide in him.

Abide means "to remain in, to stay in, to be at home in, or to be at ease with." I know many Christians have heard this text preached numerous times. I also know that when things are familiar, there is a tendency to think, "I know that! I've heard that! I've tried that to the best of my ability, but it's not working. I want to abide, but I don't know how." I understand your frustration. It's like looking at a jigsaw puzzle—seeing the picture on the box doesn't mean it's easy getting all the pieces in place.

Hopefully this chapter will move more pieces into the right place. At this point, we're ready for our character question, a question that God consistently asks his people:

> "ARE YOU ABIDING IN ME?"

It's so important to understand this question correctly. Here are the wrong questions to ask if the character of Christ is our goal:

- "Are you trying your best to change?"

- "Are you becoming a better you?"

- "Are you addressing the problem areas in your life?"

- "Are you going to counseling?"

- "Are you working enough, doing enough, or attending church enough?"

The real question from God's perspective is "Are you abiding in me?"

Apart from abiding in him, we can do nothing![9] We cannot produce spiritual fruit on our own. We cannot bring the lasting, core-level, character-alter-
ing changes that are necessary. Scripture clearly tells us that the Holy Spirit
starts the work of character change, the Holy Spirit continues the work of
character change, the Holy Spirit enables the work of character change, the
Holy Spirit produces the fruit of character change, and the Holy Spirit com-
pletes the work of character change.

Our part is to abide in him, stay with him, and rest in him. As we abide in him
by spending time with him, God does the work of character transformation.

If Christians miss this connection, they will inevitably engage in sin man-
agement instead of character development. They see the standard of Scripture and want to live up to that standard. When their own efforts fail, they
find themselves making promises to God, to friends and family, and even
to themselves. They may say something such as, "Starting tomorrow, I won't
do that again," or "I know I've messed up, but I've made a commitment to
myself to be different."

Instead of abiding and allowing the Holy Spirit to do the work, they get
impatient and try to manufacture the character of God themselves. They
try to take out the bad stuff in their lives and put in the good stuff that
the Bible commands. They enter the self-driven process of eliminating
flaws and striving for perfection. But after awhile, they begin to live behind a prison of rules and restrictions, do's and don'ts, thou shalts and
thou shalt nots.

It is a sad and disappointing life. Too many Christians have fooled themselves into thinking that with enough discipline, time, and hard work, they
could change their character. If the goal is to be a better version of ourselves, that might be enough. But that's not the goal.

God's goal is that we are transformed into the character of Christ. That goal
is not accomplished by personal effort; it is accomplished as Christians
abide in Christ. Are you abiding in Christ?

After talking to people for years on the subject of abiding, I've noticed two areas where people get stuck. First, some struggle with what it looks like to actually abide in Christ. When you wake up tomorrow, what do you do? Is a devotional time considered abiding in Christ? Is that something you do at church or in prayer?

A second concern shared by many Christians is how abiding changes character. We live in a take-charge, do-it-yourself, work-for-what-you-get type of culture. The idea of abiding seems lazy. Do we just sit and do nothing? Do we do things while abiding? How does abiding actually change a person's character?

When Jesus taught on abstract concepts, he used parables to help people understand difficult concepts. I'm not a great parable-maker, but I do have a couple of visuals to help make these ideas easier to understand.

First, think of abiding from the perspective of spending time with someone.

For any relationship to grow, you must spend time with that person. Abiding in Christ is simply spending time with God *where the focus is God*.

Take a look at how Norman Douty describes spending time with God:

> If I am to be like Him, then God in His grace must do it, and the sooner I come to recognize it the sooner I will be delivered from another form of bondage ... Forget about trying to be like Him. Instead of letting that fill your mind and heart, let Him fill it. Just behold Him, look upon Him through the Word. Come to the Word for one purpose and that is to meet the Lord. Not to get your mind crammed full of things about the sacred Word, but come to it to meet the Lord. Make it to be a medium, not of Biblical scholarship, but of fellowship with Christ.[10]

What a fantastic perspective on where our focus should be when we spend time with God. We can spend time with God in prayer, Bible study, worship, meditation, service, conversation throughout the day, and so forth. The key to abiding is to *focus on God while you're spending time with God*. The focus is not, "I want to learn the Bible," or "I want God to answer five questions," or "I need to check quiet time off my to-do list." It's possible to engage in the right activity with the wrong focus and miss the point completely. When we spend time with God, the focus is to be on God.

Second, think of abiding and character change from the perspective of close friends.

> WHEN PEOPLE SPEND TIME WITH GOD, CHANGE HAPPENS BY SIMPLY BEING WITH HIM.

When you hang out with someone for years, you start to rub off on each other. You pick up phrases and gestures they use and their likes and dislikes. Your habits change. Sometimes people even start to look like each other (especially in marriage). Gradual change happens by simply being with that person.

When people spend time with God, change happens by simply being with him. As they talk to God in prayer, meet with him in the word, and share their problems and victories with him, eventually they start to think the way he thinks and are moved by what moves him. His values become their values. His word becomes their standard. By virtue of being with him, they become like him.

Third, think of abiding and character change from the perspective of grafting trees together.

When farmers want a stronger tree, a tree that produces more fruit, or one that is more resistant to disease, they can create it through the process of grafting. Farmers take the trunk and roots of one tree and graft in the live stems of another. If the graft works, they get change that would not normally happen on its own. They get things like seedless grapes; oranges and tangerines growing on the same tree; and stronger, healthier trees that are drought resistant and immune to diseases. In other words, an ordinary tree produces abnormal results because it connects to a different source.

Jesus says, "I am the vine, you are the branches; he who abides in Me [stays connected to me] bears much fruit." As we are grafted into him, we get abnormal results because of our connection to a different source. When we try to change pride, anger, jealousy, lying, lust, addiction, or anything else, we hit a wall. But as we are connected to a different source, God has the ability to bring different results.

Fourth, think of abiding and character change from the perspective of disciplined and focused action.

Some people mistake abiding for doing nothing. They falsely assume that the options are *abide* or *do*. You can either hang out with God, or you can do something. That is not the scenario God is presenting. Abiding is about being with him and allowing him to direct the doing.

In the last chapter, I quoted G. Campbell Morgan on waiting on God. Let's read those words again:

> Waiting for God is not laziness. Waiting for God is not going to sleep. Waiting for God is not the abandonment of effort. Waiting for God means, first, activity under command; second, readiness for any new command … third, the ability to do nothing until the command is given.[11]

When you and I spend time with God, he points out the things that need to be done.

The Bible is filled with things to do. We are to pray, serve, humble ourselves, give, be good stewards, disciple others, witness our faith, provide for our families, encourage people, study to show ourselves approved, be kind, be merciful, be long-suffering, be patient, and on and on. There is plenty of doing.

The problem occurs when Christians see all of the doing as a personal challenge to fulfill the standard of God. They soon discover that they cannot do it. The doing is to flow out of being. As we are with Christ, his Spirit prompts us to action, and he empowers us to do what he has directed.

As you are spending time with God, he will point out things that need to be done. He is not saying, "Go do it yourself." He is sharing what he desires to do through you. We are to abide, listen, and respond as he directs.

Fifth, think about abiding and character change from the perspective of an employee—not a manager.

The moment we enter relationship with Christ, the believer is never removed from the position of submission. We submit to the yoke (the teachings) of Christ, and we stay in that position. Believers become frustrated when they try to regain control of their lives and run everything themselves.

But if we think of abiding from the perspective of an employee instead of a manager, we instinctively understand that our actions are to be dictated by another. As an employee, you aren't expected to come up with the programs, make the big decisions, generate new ideas, and oversee the operation. But you're also not expected to sit idly and do nothing. Your actions are dictated by the boss, but it is your responsibility to move when directed.

As you abide in Christ, God is not asking you to come up with the program of change, generate new ideas for growth in Christ, and oversee the process of character transformation. You are not the manager. The Holy Spirit is over the project. Our responsibility is to live like the employee. As God directs, we do. Yet even our doing is empowered by him.

I think now is the time for personal confession. From the time I was a kid, my mom stressed the importance of spending time daily with God in prayer and in the word. By the time I graduated from high school, I had read the Bible from cover to cover several times (the same was true of my siblings). I fell away from this habit in the first three years of college, but God brought me back to these roots in 1994.

The mid-to-late nineties were filled with an unusual passion for the things of God. During this time, I developed a system for spending time with God. In Star Trek terms, I was the equivalent of the Christian borg. I simply assimilated anything of value.

I heard a pastor speak of how Spurgeon got up every morning at 4 a.m. to be with God. I started to get up at 4 a.m. I attended a prayer conference, and Peter Lord suggested a model for prayer (praise, thanksgiving, confession, intercession, and petition). I accepted this model. A couple of years later, another prayer guru taught that prayer should be about adoration, consecration, thanksgiving, and supplication/intercession. I assimilated this model also.

One biblical teacher taught that we are to interact with the Scriptures. "Don't just read the words, interact with the text!" How do you interact with the text? Journal your thoughts under these headings: General Observations, Revelation of God, Points of Application, and Steps of Obedience. I started journaling.

Another pastor emphasized the importance of Scripture memorization. I started memorizing Scripture. Another pastor encouraged Christians to pray on your spiritual armor each day. Yes, I assimilated this too.

As you might imagine, this "devotional" thing was getting out of hand. To keep everything organized, I created a notebook with tabs. Lots of tabs. I had everything broken down by the days of the week, prayer guides, the disciple's cross, spiritual armor sheets, questions for daily living, articles on how to read God's word, journaling notes, memorization charts, and a devotional guide outline that allotted a specific portion of time for each activity. It *only* took two and a half hours to get through everything but I felt really "spiritual" (Christian code for prideful). God used one simple encounter in 2003 to change everything.

I was attending a flagship church planter's conference in north Georgia. My roommate for the conference was Vance Pitman. Vance is the pastor of our sponsoring church in Las Vegas, and we'd been friends for a while. On one morning, I got up and started my routine. I had my notebook, my tabs, my charts, my journals, my Bible, and a massive cup of coffee. Vance was asleep. I had worked my list for an hour or so when Vance finally got up. He put on his glasses, picked up his Bible, sat down in a chair, and started reading. About ten minutes later, he started crying. It might be impolite to ask another dude why he's crying in his devotional time, but curiosity got the best of me.

Vance shared how God spoke to him through a particular passage. The insights were incredible. The dialogue was real. Vance was visibly moved. *And he didn't even have a notebook!* It didn't seem right. Where were his charts and tabs and journal entries? How did he go from asleep to engaged in less than fifteen minutes?

I couldn't tell you the last time I was moved by a quiet time. I had learned a lot. I had gained information. I could check the discipline box for effort. But I was not connecting with God on a relational level.

I asked Vance to describe his devotional life. He said, "Paul, my only goal is to spend time with my Father. I simply open his word and pray to know him. Paul, it's not about religion; it's about a relationship."

God taught me an amazing lesson that morning. You can be at the right place at the right time doing the right thing and still miss the point. If the goal is to become like Christ and if the process is abiding in Christ and if Christ is to be the focus, then focus on him.

For so many years, I missed the point. I learned about God, but I didn't know him. I memorized his word, but I couldn't recognize his voice. I made the entire exercise about devotional discipline, and the whole time, he just wanted to be with me. As a result, I found myself trying to change my own character instead of Christ living his character through me.

Here's a valuable lesson from a recovering Christian borg: be careful that you don't miss the goal in the process of being "spiritual."

I cannot encourage you enough to spend focused time meditating on the truths of abiding. God's plan is not to make you a better you; God's plan is to transform your character into the character of Christ. The entire process is the work of the Holy Spirit. Our part is to abide in him.

Are you abiding in Christ? Are you resting in him? Listen to the gentle question of God.

"Are you abiding in me?"

Personal Reflection/Group Discussion

1. Are you abiding in Christ? If so, write out several ways that abiding has become a regular part of your life. If not, what challenges are keeping you from abiding in Christ?

_____

_____

_____

_____

_____

_____

_____

_____

2. When you spend time with God, is the focus on him or on you? This question does not mean to imply that we cannot share personal struggles with God. However, if the time is always spent on our wants, our needs, and our questions, we can miss the point completely. How can you discover if the focus is really on God?

_____

_____

_____

_____

_____

_____

_____

_____

3. How is God developing your character today? List several character traits of Christ that are being developed in you.

_____

_____

_____

_____

_____

_____

_____

_____

4. While it's possible for people to make minor adjustments to their habits or issues, only God can bring about long-term change. What are some areas of character that you've tried to change in your own strength? How long did the change last?

_____

_____

_____

_____

_____

_____

_____

_____

8   A Legacy Question

It's a rare thing for people to live in the present in a way that truly matters in the future. So much of our time is spent putting out fires, answering the call of the immediate, and trying to manage the menial. Some of that is necessary. Some of that is even good. But a life built around the immediate will lose the ability to selectively and purposefully invest in things that really matter.

I recently ran across an article that drove this idea home. Here's an excerpt:

> John W. Gardner, founding chairman of Common Cause, said it's a rare and high privilege to help people understand the difference they can make—not only in their own lives, but also in the lives of others, simply by giving of themselves.
>
> Gardner tells of a cheerful old man who asked the same question of just about every new acquaintance he fell into conversation with: "What have you done that you believe in and you are proud of?"
>
> He never asked conventional questions such as "What do you do for a living?" It was always, "What have you done that you believe in and are proud of?"
>
> It was an unsettling question for people who had built their self-esteem on their wealth or their family name or their exalted job title.
>
> Not that the old man was a fierce interrogator. He was delighted by a woman who answered, "I'm doing a good job raising three children;" and by a cabinetmaker who said, "I believe in good workmanship and practice it;" and by a woman who said, "I started a bookstore and it's the best bookstore for miles around."

"I don't really care how they answer," said the old man. "I just want to put the thought into their minds.

"They should live their lives in such a way that they can have a good answer. Not a good answer for me, but for themselves. That's what's important."[1]

What a fantastic thought! What have you done that you believe in and that you are proud of? It's a question that forces people to look past personal victories that have been won at the expense of others.

For example, let's say a successful businessman fully believes in the value of a huge merger. It takes two years to complete. It will establish his company strategically for another twenty years. The sense of professional accomplishment may be incredible. However, could he still be proud of the accomplishment if it costs him his family? Would it matter if the company is financially set if his marriage is completely destroyed?

What have you done that you believe in and that *you are proud of?*

In this chapter, we are asking a question that forces us to consider if our decisions are ones we are proud of. The way we answer this question affects several areas of life, including …

- **what we do and why we do it**

- **where and how much we give of ourselves, our resources, and our time**

- **the difference we make in our community and the problems we solve in the world**

- **the strength of our marriages, the unity of our churches, and our impact for the kingdom of God**

On a personal level, it is the defining issue for our development in Christ. On a church level, it has the power to turn strangers into families. Emotionally, it gives us the ability stand firm in difficult times even when we don't see God's immediate relief. When you close your eyes in death, it's the difference between leaving a legacy or just leaving.

What single question could God ask that has so much impact? I'm not sure how God will ask the question in your life, but in my life, it goes like this:

> **"WILL YOU DIE TO SELF AND SERVE OTHERS?"**

Let's see this question lived out in a biblical context, with two goals in mind. First, I want you to discover the subtle (and sometimes not-so-subtle) ways God asks this question. There are times when God prompts the question with a temporary need to fill. There are other times when God builds the question through a time of personal sacrifice and delayed dreams. Second, I want you to identify areas of your life that you believe in and are proud of. It is easier to die to self and serve others in the future when you recognize the difference those decisions have made in the past.

What kind of legacy will you leave? Let Mark 10 help you find an answer. We find the following story in verses 41–45 (NLT):

> When the ten other disciples heard what James and John had asked, they were indignant. So Jesus called them together and said, "You know that the rulers in this world lord it over their people, and officials flaunt their authority over those under them. But among you it will be different. Whoever wants to be a leader among you must be your servant, and whoever wants to be first among you must be the slave of everyone else. For even the Son of Man came not to be served but to serve others and to give his life as a ransom for many."

Do you feel as though you've entered someone else's conversation and have no idea what they're talking about? Let me fill in some details.

In this passage, Jesus has just told the disciples what will happen to him in the coming days.[2] He will go to Jerusalem; he will be delivered to the chief priests; and they will condemn him, mock him, spit upon him, scourge him, and kill him. Three days later, he will rise again.

The conversation was somber. Jesus not only described the future, he described it in brutally honest terms. Jesus fully understood that if he continued on his current path, death was waiting on the other side. Of course, we know the choice he made.

The very fact that Jesus knew what would happen and continued on the same path makes this scene one of the most selfless moments of Christ's life. Jesus was not forced on the cross. He was not beaten into submission by the Roman guards. He was not unexpectedly jumped by an angry mob when he entered Jerusalem's gates. He knowingly, willfully, and selflessly walked the path that would lead to his death. That thought is crucial for the next scene.

As soon as Jesus finishes speaking, James and John (two of his disciples) pull Jesus off to the side and say, "We want You to do for us whatever we ask of You … Grant that we may sit, one on Your right and one on Your left, in Your glory."[3]

In our society, unless you're dealing with seating assignments for a wedding reception, where a person sits at dinner may not be a huge issue. However, in first-century Jewish life, the seats next to a leader were places of honor and authority. In some cases, the person on the right side was given honor, dignity, and authority equal to the leader. We are not sure of their exact intentions, but it is clear that James and John wanted to be elevated by Christ.

Bear in mind, Jesus had just described the horrific details of his death, and James and John are essentially saying, "Before you die, will you promise to leave your most prized possessions to us?" The selfishness of James and John is stunning.

Jesus handled the situation better than I would have. If I were God in human flesh, I would have dropped some Volkswagen-sized hailstones on a couple of rude disciples, but then again, that's why he's God and I'm not. Anyway, he told them that those positions were not his to give and that the Father already had plans for those positions.

Take that information, and just hold on to it for a moment. This question might seem odd, but I promise there's a point. To what extent (or in what ways) do you want to be like Jesus? Another way of asking the same question would be, what part of Jesus' life would you like to see manifest in yours?

If you've never thought about that question, or if you're having trouble getting your mind around the concept, let me get you started:

- **Do you want to be like Jesus in his demeanor or his heart for people?**

- **Do you want to be like Jesus in his wisdom, his overall character, or his unlimited power?**

- **Are you drawn to his ability to commune with the Father, his miraculous abilities, or his overall holiness?**

To what extent (or in what ways) do you want to be like Jesus?

It's one thing to pray, "God, make me like Christ. God, help me to be like Jesus. God, I want to be more like you." All of that sounds good, but I wonder if God is in heaven saying, "Which part? Do you want to be like me in my love and compassion, or do you want to be like me in my service to others and my willingness to endure the cross?" To be like Christ in Mark 10 indicates a willingness to die to self and serve others. It's important that Christians see the fullness of what it means to become like Christ. Yes, we have a desire to become like Christ in his character. But do we have the same desire to become like Christ in his suffering?

Being transformed into the image of Christ does not come in one installment of "Awesomeness." It comes through moment-by-moment removal and instilling. God removes the remnants of the flesh so that the fullness of our nature in Christ can shine through.

But here's the great news! If you want to join God in this transformation of your character, you don't have to wait. You don't have to keep praying and hoping that God will do something. You don't have to beg Jesus to put you on the path to Christ-likeness. You and I are already on the path. The opportunities for transformation are all around us. We are not waiting on God to teach the lesson; God is waiting on us to enter the classroom.

The lesson is summarized in one question: "Will you die to self and serve others?" If our desire is to be like Christ, then listen carefully as he tells us how to get there: "For even the Son of Man did not come to be served, but to serve."[4] Jesus served others. He did not come as a leader of leaders. He came as the servant of all. If you really want to be like Christ, I've got some great news. Starting now, you can be a servant.

Look back at Mark 10:43b–45, which says,

> But whoever wishes to become great among you shall be your servant; and whoever wishes to be first among you shall be slave of all. For even the Son of Man did not come to be served, but to serve, and to give His life a ransom for many.

Jesus was constantly turning the disciples' worldview upside down. Now he flips their view of greatness. From the world's perspective, the higher your position, the greater you are. The more prestige you have, the more honor and respect you generate. From God's perspective, honor does not come by how many people you oversee but by how many people you serve. *"Whoever wishes to be first among you shall be slave of all."*

That is not to say that Christians should reject positions of leadership. Everyone (Christian and non-Christian) should work hard and take the opportunities afforded to them. The Bible is filled with godly people who were placed in incredible positions of leadership:

- **Moses led an estimated three million people out of bondage.**

- **Joseph was second-in-command to pharaoh.**

- **David and Solomon were kings.**

- **Daniel played a prominent role in the king's court.**

- **Esther was queen.**

The Bible does not discourage Christians from accepting positions of leadership. It simply means that with greater responsibility comes greater service. As a leader, God gives you a greater platform, greater resources, and greater opportunities. When the blessings come and you are in the position to make a difference, the question remains, "Will you die to self and serve others?"

When people answer yes to this question, it's not a one-time yes. It is a regular, ongoing, everyday decision to die to self and serve others. When they say yes, it generates change that ripples through the person, through families, through communities, and even through the world.

People long to see selfless living. We are drawn to stories where people of prominence use their platforms to serve others. We are moved by stories of everyday people who tackle big problems just for the sake of making a difference. Selfless living draws people together. It helps us live for something bigger than ourselves. It gives us perspective that we would have missed.

Mother Teresa said, "Let us touch the dying, the poor, the lonely, and the unwanted according to the graces we have received and let us not be ashamed or slow to do the humble work." Mother Teresa's legacy is not how quickly she ascended the ranks in the church. Her legacy is how many hurting and forgotten people she served in India.

Albert Schweitzer said, "I don't know what your destiny will be, but one thing I do know: the only ones among you who will be really happy are those who have sought and found how to serve." Schweitzer won the Nobel Prize in 1952. He was a doctor, a theologian, and an accomplished musician. But his legacy was not framed in those accomplishments. He was known for founding and sustaining the Albert Schweitzer Hospital in west and central Africa.

Dietrich Bonhoeffer said, "When Jesus calls a man, he bids him, 'Come and die.' " Bonhoeffer held a doctorate and was a distinguished professor and pastor (and a founding member of the Confessing Church). Yet he died at the age of thirty-nine in the Flossenbürg concentration camp because of his participation in the German Resistance Movement against Nazism. His accomplishments were great, but his legacy is seen in his willingness to die for those who didn't have a voice.

When Jesus says, "Whoever wishes to become great among you shall be your servant," he is not commending a way different from the way he took. He led the way. After reading the biblical accounts, we understand that no one took Jesus' life. He voluntarily laid it down. Jesus told his disciples that he could ask the Father, and the Father would send 10,000 angels to take up his cause.[5] But he didn't. He showed the world that he had the power to calm storms, to walk on water, to heal the sick, and to raise the dead, and yet he chose to die in order to serve others.[6]

We could share countless more quotes and stories of people who are well-known and unknown but who devoted their lives to others. Each story moves us in a different way. In each story, we are compelled to think, "If I were in that position, what would I do?"

> TODAY, IN WHATEVER SITUATION YOU'RE IN, WILL YOU DIE TO SELF AND SERVE OTHERS?

Ironically, God will ask you a lot of questions, but that's not one of them. It's not about what you would do if you were someone else. It's not about what you would do if you were in that same situation. It's about what you will do in the place where God has positioned you. Today, in whatever situation you're in, will you die to self and serve others?

When our church was getting started, we would serve breakfast to motorists as a way of getting the word out. In our first several years, we served tens of thousands of motorists on multiple occasions. Through the help of mission teams and core members, we would set up at an intersection at about 7 a.m. We would hand out bottles of fruit juice. We would give a breakfast bar and an invite card.

The conversations we had with people were amazing. There would be a number of people who would say, "This is an answer to my prayers. I've been looking for a church. You guys are right around the corner. We'll see you Sunday." When our team would meet after the distributions, there would be fifteen or twenty similar stories. We would get so excited.

Immediately, I would get the word out to key people in the church. I would say, "Be prepared for Sunday because there's going to be a whole group of new people. We just finished handing out breakfast at several intersections, and God really blessed our time. Make sure Kids' Life is ready, make sure we have enough bulletins, make sure to buy extra donuts. It's going to be great."

Here's the funny part. When people said, "This is an answer to my prayers. I'll see you on Sunday," I thought they meant, "This is an answer to my prayers, and I'll see you on Sunday." Yet Sunday would come, and none of these people would show up.

We would serve breakfast again. Same response. "This is an answer to my prayers. I'll see you on Sunday." We would rally the troops. "God blessed our distribution time. Make sure Kids' Life is ready, make sure we have enough bulletins, make sure to buy extra donuts. It's going to be great." Sunday would roll around, and none of these people would come.

We did this over and over. After a while, when people said, "This is an answer to my prayers. I'll see you Sunday," I wanted to say, "Whatever! Just eat your breakfast and don't be late for work." I was cynical because no one ever came!

Then one day, I'm standing on this street corner with juice bottles in one hand and breakfast bars in the other. I'm thinking about all the time and money we've put into serving breakfast and the fact that no one ever came. In my mind, I'm telling God that this is a waste of time and resources. Right in the middle of my speech, God spoke one question into my heart: "Would you still serve people even if you knew they would never come?"

I wanted to argue with him. "But God, you called us to start a church—not a breakfast distribution service! But God, we don't have the money to keep this up. This takes too much time. It's a lot of work to get everything together. We're running out of mission teams. But God, shouldn't we do something that's more effective?" God didn't waver on his question. "Would you still serve people even if you knew they would never come?"

At the heart of his question was an important distinction. "Paul, are you distributing breakfast because you love people or because you want to use them? Are you actually concerned about who you're serving, or are you just trying to get someone to fill a seat? Paul, will you die to self and die to your plans and die to your agenda and simply serve people with no strings attached? What is it going to be? Will you die to self and serve others?"

Standing on a street corner with breakfast in my hand and cars zooming past on both sides, God taught me an incredible lesson. Praise God, he uses the ordinary to teach the eternal. Praise God, he teaches as we go. Praise God, he asks questions that irritate the conscience to the point that we chase after him for relief. I might have gotten run over in his classroom but I'll never forget the lesson.

When I could honestly say yes to God's question, there was a renewed joy in serving people. I wasn't serving them to get something back. I just wanted to serve.

I even became convicted for handing out church invitations with the breakfast, so we told all of our people to put them in their pockets but to not hand them out with breakfast. We let them know that our goal was not to get people to our church. It was about letting people know that God cares.

People would drive up and ask, "What's this about?" We would say, "We're just a church in the neighborhood that wants to be a blessing to the community." That's it. We wouldn't give the name of the church. We didn't hand them an invitation. We were completely content to just serve them under the banner of Christ's church and not our local assembly.

Some people would say, "That's great," and drive on. Others wanted to know more. If they requested information, we would give them a card. If not, they went on their way, and we went on ours.

God was using multiple situations like this to bring me back to this question. The opportunities for dying to self and serving others were all around me:

- **When people were coming over to the house and Brea was cooking and cleaning and my ball game was on TV, I had a choice: Will I hit record, die to self, and serve others?**

- **When I was tired in the evening and just wanted to fall asleep in front of the TV and my daughter asked, "Daddy, do you want to play Lego's with me?", I had a choice: Will I die to self, and serve others?**

- **When help was needed with the children's ministry, or when more counseling needed to be done, or when more meetings crept in on "my" time, the question remained: Will I die to self and serve others?**

Every day God allows us to see multiple moments where we can say no to self and yes to service. Does this mean that you never take time to do things you enjoy or to rest? Of course not! Every night Jesus went to sleep, and there was more work to do. Jesus simply followed the promptings of the Father and served out of the overflow of that relationship.

That last statement is so crucial. Jesus served out of the overflow of his relationship with the Father. If you do not answer this question in the

> JESUS SERVED OUT OF THE OVERFLOW OF HIS RELATIONSHIP WITH THE FATHER.

context of your relationship with God, you will gain a "Messiah complex" that feeds self instead of denies it. We can fool ourselves into thinking that if it's going to be done, I have to do it. I have to be involved. I have to take on every challenge. I have to meet every demand. I, I, I ...

Every fight is not your fight, and every need is not your burden to bear. But it can be so easy to be consumed with our plans, our time, and our dreams that we miss the big point: God's plan is not to fulfill your every dream;

God's plan is to conform you and I into the image of Christ.[7] Jesus says, "For even the Son of Man did not come to be served, but to serve, and to give His life a ransom for many." Are you willing to open up the schedule of your life, your dreams, and your agenda and say, "God, I'm willing to die to self and serve others"?

As we finish this chapter, I want to leave you with three thoughts that I've stumbled across while wrestling with the legacy question.

You die to self daily (in many ways), not in a moment (through one big event).

Take the opportunities that God brings to you. You don't need to go on a big quest for service. Just look for the opportunities he brings across your path.

The normal flow of life will lead toward death to self.

When you're a kid, others do for you. When you're single, you live and make decisions for self. When you get married, two become one. You die to your way, money, and plans. It becomes our life, our money, and our plans. When you have kids, it's no longer your sleep, your free time, and your sports car. It becomes my child's needs, our family time, and a spacious (yet stylish) means of transportation. The further you go in life, the more the normal flow of life leads toward death to self.

A legacy worth leaving is comprised of a thousand little yeses to God's continual question, "Will you die to self and serve others?"

Imagine what God could do through a local church if the people just said, "Yes, Lord! Bring us the hurting. We're willing to serve them. Open our eyes to see the things that burden your heart. God, where is the church falling short? Who can we love? How can we be involved?"

Ralph Barton, a top cartoonist, left this note pinned to his pillow before taking his own life: "I have had few difficulties, many friends, great successes; I have gone from wife to wife, from house to house, visited great countries of the world, but I am fed up with inventing devices to fill up twenty-four hours of the day."

If life is only about us, we are simply inventing devices to fill up twenty-four hours of the day. Jesus taught his disciples that life was not about them. Life truly happens when we are willing to die to self and serve others. How much life are you missing out on today?

Personal Reflection/Group Discussion

1. "What have you done that you believe in and are proud of?"

_____

_____

_____

_____

_____

_____

_____

2. In what areas is God asking you the question, "Will you die to self and serve others?"

_____

_____

_____

_____

_____

_____

_____

3. What is a burden that he's placed on your heart, but you've been responding to with, "Not today"?

_____

_____

_____

_____

_____

4. How are you following the example of Christ? In what ways are you serving others?

_____

_____

_____

_____

_____

5. How can you serve your spouse? How can you say no to self and invest in your children?

_____

_____

_____

_____

_____

Conclusion

As *8 Questions* comes to an end, I want to take a moment to review the path we've traveled and share a few thoughts on the path you will be taking.

We started this book with two concepts essential to learning. First, every teacher is different. Second, there is no way that a teacher can adjust to the learning style of every student, so you must adjust to their styles of teaching if you want to be a successful student. When students do not make that adjustment, they fall behind in class, receive poor grades, and experience a semester that seems to last for an eternity.

We applied these concepts to the path of Christian discipleship. We see throughout the Gospels that Jesus is referred to as *rabbi* or *teacher*. With Jesus as rabbi, we become his disciples and students. Subsequently, much of our relationship with him will be spent in the process of learning.

By connecting what it takes to be a good student in general to the biblical model of discipleship, we were left with an interesting thought: If every teacher is different, and if you must adjust to your teacher's style, how well are you adapting to the style of our ultimate teacher Jesus Christ?

Understanding the teaching style of Christ (and adjusting to that style) can be the difference between enjoying a vibrant relationship with him and struggling through religious duties performed out of obligation. It can be the difference between receiving answers and simply hearing silence. In fact, this question may be at the core of so much of the frustration, anxiety, and relational tension we feel between us and God.

Therefore, we must ask, what is the teaching style of Christ? Through an overview of the Gospels, we discovered that Jesus used questions as a primary teaching tool. He constantly asked questions, and God still uses questions to teach us. When our ears are tuned to hear his questions, they actually guide us to God's answers.

These questions, written from God's perspective, capture the heart of this book. They linger in our minds and profoundly shape our beliefs and actions when we understand them. The questions God asks are,

- *A Relational Question.* **Will you pursue me in the process of whatever you're going through?**

- *A Faith Question.* **Will you trust me?**

- *A Grace Question.* **Are you depending on yourself or on me?**

- *A Contentment Question.* **When will Jesus be enough?**

- *A Control Question.* **What have I asked you to do?**

- *A Patience Question.* **Will you wait on me?**

- *A Character Question.* **Are you abiding in me?**

- *A Legacy Question.* **Will you die to self and serve others?**

I've shared several times throughout this book that the wording of the questions changes from person to person but the essence will be the same. You may be able to identify with some or all of the questions in this book. You may have dozens of other questions that God has been asking you. Regardless of the specific questions, my prayer is that what you've learned in this book gives you a glimpse of how God faithfully works to draw us to himself even when his answers are slow to come. Every day is a new adventure with God. Every day is an opportunity to walk with your rabbi, learn from him, listen to him, serve him, and experience him. The ultimate goal is not to have *our* questions answered but rather to enjoy an abiding, living, vibrant relationship with Jesus Christ.

Remember, everything God desires to do in and through your life, he will accomplish out of the overflow of your relationship with him. Everything! When he works on your character, he does it out of the overflow of your relationship. When he works on your marriage, friendships, and fears, his work begins in your relationship with him. When he guides your life, answers your prayers, and yes, even asks you questions, it happens in your relationship.

So where do we go from here? Our responsibility is to abide in him—to run to him, be with him, and listen to him. As we abide, God guides. Then when God whispers those lingering questions in your mind, consider it an invitation for dialogue. Your rabbi may be a different kind of teacher, but you can adjust to and learn from his style.

May God bless you as you walk with and *learn to hear* Christ!

Appendix

Introduction
1. Mark 8:32b–33

The Teaching Style of Our Rabbi
1. Mark 1:22
2. Matthew 7:28
3. Matthew 21:15
4. Matthew 21:16
5. Mark 4:34 (NLT)
6. Matthew 13:34
7. Matthew 6:26
8. Matthew 22:19–21
9. Mark 3:33
10. Matthew 16:13
11. Matthew 19:17
12. Matthew 8:26
13. Matthew 9:28
14. Matthew 6:27
15. Luke 22:27

1: A Relational Question
1. Mark 8:32b–33

2: A Faith Question
1. Genesis 22:1–19
2. Joshua 6
3. Daniel 6:16–28
4. Luke 9:23–27

5. Matthew 8:5–13

6. Numbers 32:23

7. Matthew 6:24

8. John 16:33

9. 1 Peter 3:14

10. Genesis 5:21–24

11. Genesis 15:1–6

12. Genesis 12:1–4

13. Genesis 17:17 and 21:5

14. Hebrews 11:11

15. Job 38:1–3 (NIV)

16. Job 42:3–5 (NIV)

3: A Grace Question

1. Author unknown, *"Illustrations concerning grace."* Sermon Illustrations:
http://www.sermonillustrations.com/a-z/g/grace.htm (December 2011).

2. Romans 6:23

3. 2 Corinthians 12:8–9

4. Hebrews 4:16

5. Acts 20:32

6. Watchman Nee, *The Normal Christian Life* (Wheaton: Tyndale House, 1956), 155.

7. 2 Timothy 4:7

8. 2 Timothy 1:4

9. 2 Timothy 1:5–7

10. 2 Timothy 1:8

11. 2 Corinthians 11:23–28; Acts 28:3; and 2 Timothy 4:16

12. 1 Timothy 5:23

13. 2 Timothy 1:9

14. Ephesians 2:8–9

15. Romans 7:14–8:8

16. Romans 8:28–30

17. Zechariah 4:6

18. 2 Timothy 4:7

19. Proverbs 3:5–6

20. James 4:6

4: A Contentment Question

1. Genesis 24:35
2. Deuteronomy 6:10–12
3. 1 Samuel 18:14–15
4. 2 Chronicles 1:11–12
5. Luke 12:15 (ESV)
6. 1 Timothy 6:9 (ESV)
7. Matthew 6:24 (ESV)
8. Psalm 16:11 (ESV)
9. Psalm 17:15 (ESV)
10. Hebrews 13:5 (ESV)
11. Romans 7:14–26 and Romans 7:7
12. Philippians 3:6
13. Acts 7:54–8:3
14. Acts 9:3–4
15. Galatians 1:15–24
16. Galatians 2:1–2
17. Proverbs 5:21; 16:33; 20:24; and 21:1
18. Colossians 3:4
19. Philippians 4:13 (emphasis mine)
20. Psalm 73:25 (NLT)

5: A Control Question

1. Author unknown, *"The Serenity Prayer." Terry M:*
   http://www.winternet.com/~terrym/serenity.html (February 2012).
2. 2 Corinthians 5:17
3. 1 Corinthians 6:19–20
4. Galatians 2:20
5. Nehemiah 9:6; Acts 17:24; and Hebrews 11:3
6. Proverbs 21:1
7. Genesis 8:22; Psalm 31:15; and Daniel 2:21
8. Amos 4:7 and Matthew 5:45
9. Psalm 75:6–7
10. Philippians 4:7

6: A Patience Question

1. Psalm 21; 25:5; 27:14; and 37:9
2. Psalm 130:5
3. Psalm 37:7
4. Psalm 62:5
5. 1 Samuel 17:10
6. 1 Samuel 17:22
7. 1 Samuel 17:34–36
8. 1 Samuel 17:32
9. 2 Samuel 5:6–25; 6:1–15; and 8:1–18
10. 2 Samuel 11:1–4
11. 2 Samuel 11:14–27
12. Psalm 35:6; 55:15; 58:6; 69:28; and 109:8
13. 1 Chronicles 22
14. Richard Wurmbrand, *Tortured for Christ* (Bartlesville: Living Sacrifice Book Company, 1967).
15. G. Campbell Morgan, *"Illustrations concerning waiting on God."* Sermon Illustrations: http://www.sermonillustrations.com/a-z/w/waiting_on_god.htm (March 2012).

7: A Character Question

1. 1 Corinthians 6:19
2. Philippians 1:6
3. Philippians 2:12b–13
4. Romans 6:23
5. 2 Corinthians 3:18 (NLT)
6. Psalm 86:12; Isaiah 24:15; Mark 2:12; and Luke 2:20
7. Romans 3:23; Psalm 8:1; John 11:40; and Exodus 24:17
8. Galatians 5:22–23
9. John 15:5
10. Miles Stanford, *The Complete Green Letters* (Grand Rapids: Zondervan, 1983).
11. G. Campbell Morgan, *"Illustrations concerning waiting on God."* Sermon Illustrations: http://www.sermonillustrations.com/a-z/w/waiting_on_god.htm (March 2012).

8: A Legacy Question

1. Dr. Dale E. Turner, *"Illustrations concerning purpose." Sermon Illustrations:* http://www.sermonillustrations.com/a-z/p/purpose.htm (March 2012).

2. Mark 10:32–34

3. Mark 10:35 and 37

4. Mark 10:45

5. Matthew 26:53

6. Mark 4:35–41; Matthew 14:22–34; Mark 2:1–13; and John 11:1–44

7. Romans 8:29

CPSIA information can be obtained at www.ICGtesting.com
Printed in the USA
BVOW031908051112

304592BV00004BA/1/P